THE TORAH UNIVERSE

SEASONS OF LIFE

The Reflection of the Jewish Year
in the Natural World

THE TORAH UNIVERSE

SEASONS OF LIFE

The Reflection of the Jewish Year
in the Natural World

Nosson Slifkin

TARGUM PRESS
MISHNAS RISHONIM

Published by:
Targum Press, Inc.
22700 W. Eleven Mile Rd.
Southfield, MI 48034
in conjuction with:
Mishnas Rishonim

Distributed by:
Feldheim Publishers
200 Airport Executive Park
Nanuet, NY 10954

Distributed in Israel by:
Targum Press
POB 43170
Jerusalem 91430

Printed in Israel

Photo credits: Author (cover, pp. 74, 86, 99, 107, 120, 203, 211); The Tisch Family Zoological Gardens (pp. 93, 130, 208); Israel Government Press Office (pp. 73, 79, 103, 143, 223); Corel CD Photo Gallery (pp. 95, 117, 139, 147, 153, 171, 195, 206, 242, 244); Benjamin Hassan (p. 150).

This work is dedicated by
Rabbi and Mrs. Joseph Katz
in memory of their beloved parents

לעילוי נשמת
ר׳ ישראל אלתר ב״ר יוסף הכהן ז״ל
פעסי בת ר׳ צבי ע״ה
ר׳ שמעון ב״ר אורי שראגא ז״ל

And their beloved uncle and aunt
לע״נ החבר ברוך ב״ר יעקב ז״ל
יהודית בת שלמה ע״ה

ת.נ.צ.ב.ה.

מדרש שמואל

ישיבה גדולה
וכולל אברכים

בנשיאות:
הגאון הרב שמואל אויערבאך
שליט"א

ראש הישיבה:
הרב בנימין מושקוביץ שליט"א

מנהל הישיבה:
הרב משה ויסלובסקי שליט"א

שכ' שערי חסד
ת"ד 7345
ירושלים 91072

המשרד:
רח' אבן שפרוט 3
טל. 4515 566 02
פקס: 5723 566 02

MIDRASH SHMUEL

Talmudical College &
Institute for Advanced
Torah Studies

Patron:
Rabbi Shmuel Auerbach

Rosh HaYeshiva:
Rabbi Binyomin Moskovits

Director:
Rabbi Moshe Wislowsky

3 Ibn Shaprut St.
Jerusalem 91072
Tel: (02) 566 4515
Fax: (02) 566 5723

כ"ג שבט תשנ"ח

ידידי המחבר נתן סליפקין נ"י, הלומד אצלינו הרבה שנים בשקידה עצומה, הראה לי ספרו החדש בענין נפלאות הבורא המשנה עתים ומחליף את הזמנים, בחשבון מדויק .עד בלי תכלית. והצצתי זעיר שם וזעיר שם.

וכבר איתמחי גברא לכתוב באופן ברור ומעמיק לפי השקפה נכונה אשר רוח חכמים נוחה הימנה, הן בעניני גופא דגמרא, והן בעניני דרוש, וכבר זכו ספריו להתקבל ברעוא בקרב אחינו בני ישראל הקוראים בשפת אנגלית.

ועיין בדברי המחצית השקל שכ' באו"ח תס"ח סע' י' שכתב "ונודע דבכל הזמנים שאירע לאבותינו ענין כשיגיעו זמן ההוא שוב מתעורר קצת מעין הענין ההוא". ונראה לבאר דאין זה רק משום אותו ענין שאירע שגרם שחותמו המיוחד יהא מוטבע על אותו יום מכאן ואילך, אלא באותו ענין שאירע מעיד על יחודיות סגולת אותו היום אשר היא אפשרה שתגרם אותו הענין. וע"כ חוזרת ונערת אותו הסגולה בכל שנה. ונראה דדבר זה הוי בין בעניינים מיוחדים וניסים גלויים וכן במחזור התמידי של כל עניני השנה, המתחלפים לפי שנויי הטבע של הזמנים ההם.

והמעיין בספר זה בודאי יזכה אי"ה לראות באספקלריא המאירה את יופי התורה וסדר הבריאה, והקשר בין המצוות ושנויי הטבע של כל הזמן ותקופה. ועי"ז יזכה הקורא לתוספת התפעלות בגדלות הבורא יתב' ולעלות מעלה מעלה במעלות יראת שמים ואהבת ה' ותורתו. וכן יוכל לכוון עבודתו יותר לפי סגולות הזמן כאשר יכיר מה הן.

הכו"ח לכבוד התורה ולומדי'

Rabbi Leib Heyman

HaGra Shul, Bayit Vegan

103 Bayit Vegan St., Jerusalem
Tel: 642 0052

אריה לייב היימן

רב בית הכנסת "הגר"א"
בשכונת בית וגן, ירושלים עיה"ק ת"ו

רחוב בית וגן 103
טל' 642 0052

ג' מנחם אב תשנ"ז

Seasons of Life is a classical work uncovering the natural world that lies within our Holy Torah.

The highly talented author has produced an outstanding work of encyclopedic proportions. He brings to life scenes of untold natural beauty as he describes the order of the months of the Jewish calendar year, the events and the all-encompassing activities of the seasons. Using the Torah as his guiding light he demonstrates what Chazal have taught, "Hashem looked into the Torah and created the world." The Torah is alive, it is an *eitz chaim*, the blueprint of all that Hashem created. The author's purpose for writing this book was to teach this fundamental axiom.

Herein lies a voluminous world of wisdom. It is written with unusual clarity and is stimulating and enlightening. As you read, your heart, your mind and your soul, are overwhelmed by the Creator's unfathomable universe and the depths of the Torah which hint to it.

Seasons of Life may be read for pleasure and enjoyment. It will benefit the student, the layman and the *talmid chacham*. However, in order to be absorbed and thoroughly understood it must be studied in depth, and the effort is well rewarded many times over.

With Torah blessings,

Sincerely,

Leib Heyman

Letter of approbation from Rabbi Aaron Lopianski

Rosh Beis HaMedrash,

Yeshivah of Greater Washington

The Jewish year is a melody of many harmonies, each existing in its own octave, yet all reinforcing each other, producing a glorious symphony of meanings. The agricultural cycle coincides with the historical cycle, which in turn expresses itself in the *halachic* cycle.

Nosson Slifkin has produced an excellent work which takes a big step towards integrating all these various elements. It is rich in content, delightful in exposition, and inspiring in spirit.

Aaron Lopianski

CONTENTS

ACKNOWLEDGMENTS

This book developed concurrently with a series of lectures I delivered at the Acheinu Bnei Yisrael shul in Bayit Vegan. When I began the project, it was clear that it would be somewhat elaborate, but I had little idea of just how much that would be so. During the years of its preparation it proved to be extraordinarily complex, far more than anything else I had ever attempted. That it managed to reach completion is due to the generous efforts of many worthy people.

As always, I cannot adequately express my gratitude to my *rosh yeshivah*, HaGaon HaRav Binyomin Moskovits, *shlita*. His transmission of an intellectually honest approach to Gemara is of no less importance for studying material of the nature contained in this book. To the extent that I have succeeded in analyzing the Torah's approach to the Jewish year, the credit is due to him. I am grateful, too, for his support and encouragement with this and other projects.

I have greatly benefited from the *shiurim* of HaGaon HaRav Moshe Shapiro, *shlita*, some of which inspired sections of this book. I am also grateful for his encouragement of this project.

A number of distinguished *talmidei chachamim* contributed valuable material, read and revised sections of the manuscript, and offered critical advice and encouragement. I am deeply indebted to HaGaon HaRav Tzvi Kushelevsky, HaGaon HaRav Leib Hymen, Rabbi Aryeh Carmell, Rabbi Menachem Farber, Rabbi Yisroel Cohen, Rabbi Meir Tribitz, Rabbi Aaron Lopiansky, Rabbi Akiva Tatz, Rabbi Moshe Rabinowitz, and Rabbi Yehoshua Honigwachs for all their help.

One of the most enjoyable aspects of working on this material were the endless hours spent in discussion with Rabbi Amos Luban. His holistic perspective and deep sensitivity to the subject matter were invaluable. It is thanks to him that the book is able to explore the larger patterns in the year.

Rabbi Dovid Trevor painstakingly reviewed the manuscript with me, word by word. His constructive insights and incisive suggestions greatly improved this work. Thanks, too, to all those others who helped with reviewing portions of the manuscript, especially Shmully Myers.

Rabbi Yisroel Shaw demonstrated his customary expertise with his excellent editing of this book, along with perceptive criticisms. Many thanks for his professional work.

It was a privilege and pleasure to deliver this material in the Acheinu Bnei Yisrael shul, otherwise known as "The American Minyan," in Bayit VeGan. Many thanks to Rabbi Yehoshua Freilich and Rabbi Yaakov Iskowits for providing me with this invaluable forum.

My friends and colleagues in the *kollel* and yeshivah of Midrash Shmuel were a superb source of advice, perceptive insights, and encouragement, not to mention providing a sounding board for the material. Thanks also to Dr. Joel Kaye, who advised me on mat-

ACKNOWLEDGMENTS

ters of biology, as did Dr. Joel Greenberg on chaos mathematics.

Director Shai Doron and zoologist Shmulik Yedvab at the Tisch Family Zoological Gardens (the Biblical zoo) generously placed the zoo's resources at my disposal, including their photographic archives. Neot Kedumim, the Biblical Landscape Reserve, provided a wonderful opportunity to learn about the agricultural cycle and flora of the Torah. I recommend both of these magnificent places to anyone seeking to understand the animals and plants described in the Torah and to anyone who wants to enjoy the natural beauty described in this book.

Targum Press deserves an accolade for their superb handling of a highly complex production. Many thanks to Rabbi Moshe Dombey for his enthusiasm and supervision of the entire process, Akiva Atwood for the typesetting, D. Liff for the graphics work, Suri Brand for the copyediting and proofreading. May they enjoy continued success in their efforts to disseminate Torah to the English-speaking world.

My heartfelt gratitude is extended to my parents, Professor Michael and Marietta Slifkin. Aside from the obvious, they instilled in me the three qualities essential for writing this book: a love for nature, a love for wisdom, and a love for writing. May their retirement in Yerushalayim bring them continued *nachas* from their children and grandchildren.

Finally, I humbly express my gratitude to the *Ribbono shel olam* for creating a beautiful world, a wonderful Torah with which to understand it, and for enabling me to produce this work.

N. S.

Bayit VeGan, Jerusalem 5758

HOW TO USE THIS BOOK

The Introduction sets the tone for the book, explaining the basic thesis.

Part 1, "Concerning Time," explains the theory of time upon which the book is based, the structure of the calendar, and some of the patterns that are explored.

Part 2, "Within Time," is the main section of the book, covering the duration of the year. This section must be read in sequence from Nissan through Adar. Each month will be fully understood only in the context of the entire process of the year, beginning in Nissan. After reading through the whole section, one will benefit from reviewing the appropriate subsection during the relevant month.

The appendices expand on some of the ideas contained earlier in the book, but they are more speculative and of a more technical nature.

The time cycles replace the time lines found in traditional history books, for reasons that are made clear in part 1. They provide a graphical means of understanding the patterns described in the book.

Throughout the book, the small paragraphs at the side of the text contain additional information related to the concepts in the main text but not central to their flow.

INTRODUCTION

Beautiful World

The universe fills us with wonder. We are astounded by its complexity, astonished at its design, overwhelmed by its beauty. Contemplation of the universe is of great importance. It is the most accessible way of verifying the existence of God.[1] In fact, it is considered an obligation.[2] Man's ability to study the universe sets him apart from all the other creatures, and he should take advantage of this unique capability.[3] We are instructed to contemplate the skies and draw the inevitable conclusion:

"The heavens speak of Hashem's glory, and the sky tells of His handiwork" (Tehillim 19:2).

> *Lift your eyes upon high and perceive Who created these!*
> (Yeshayahu 40:26)

Examining the remarkable design of the universe not only provides us with evidence of Hashem's existence. It also enables us to improve in our service of Hashem. The increased awareness of His greatness encourages us to dedicate ourselves to Him more fully. Through contemplation of the design inherent in the universe, we increase our love toward Hashem and our awe of Him:

> This honored and awesome God, it is a mitzvah to love Him and to fear Him... And how does one come to love

and fear Him? When man contemplates the great wonders of His deeds and creations, and he perceives from them His boundless and infinite wisdom, instantly he loves and praises and gives glory, and he has a great desire to know Hashem... And when he contemplates these matters, he instantly recoils and is in awe, and he knows that he is a small, dismal, lowly creature, standing with a minuscule weakness of intellect before the Perfect Wisdom...

(Rambam, *Hilchos Yesodei HaTorah* 2:1–2)

Intellect and Emotion

The duty to perceive Hashem by studying the universe can be fulfilled by using one's intellect to discover the remarkable intricacy and complexity present in the world. For example, we can learn about the nature of the chameleon's remarkable ability to change color or the extraordinary mechanism of the human eye. Putting our mind to this task fills us with profound love and awe for the One Who created such an amazing design.

The chameleon can change its pattern as well as its color. It can also point its eyes in opposite directions.

There is, however, a downside to this method. A poet of the last century complained that scientists, if given a chance, would "unweave a rainbow." He was concerned that too much stress on analyzing natural phenomena would cause one to miss out on perceiving their beauty. His worries were justified. The increased focus on the scientific manner of viewing the world has desensitized us to the beauty of Hashem's creations. Add to this the abundance of information and imagery which constantly bombards us in this age of mass media, and the result is emotional numbness.

We need to learn to take the information we already have and increase our sensitivity to it.[4] We all know that trees produce fruit — we can either take it for granted or appreciate the miracle involved. The thrill we felt as a child when touching a leaf for the first time or seeing a bird flying through the air should not be lost to us as we grow older. It is not a matter of thinking about the detail involved. It is a question of learning to *appreciate* the beauty of nature. Such contemplation will surely bring one to a greater awareness and love for the Creator.

Beautiful Torah

So far, we have described how one can perceive proof of a Creator and attain love for Him through reflecting on the beauty and complexity of the natural world. But one can also attain these through contemplating the beauty of Torah:

> It says, *And you shall love Hashem your God with all your heart* (Devarim 6:5), but we do not know how to love Hashem! Therefore it says, *And these words which I am commanding you today shall be on your heart* (ibid., 6) — place these words on your heart, for from this you will recognize Hashem and cleave to His ways.[5]
>
> (*Sifri, Va'eschanan* 8)

Serious contemplation of the Torah leads one both to recognize that it was written by Hashem[6] and to feel love and a desire to draw near to Him. It accomplishes this in several ways. First of all, there is the sheer overwhelming complexity of the Torah, with all the richness of its interweaving patterns and the harmony of the overall structure. This causes the Torah student to gasp in amazement at Hashem's wisdom.

Second, one cannot help but be in awe of the utter perfection of the lifestyle ordained by the Torah.[7] The laws of speech are delineated in fine detail so that no harmful effects will result from one's conversation. Charity is expected from every Jew, rich or poor. One must bless Hashem before and after eating and thereby learn to appreciate his partaking of this world. The Torah deals with every single aspect of one's life, from prayer to attending to one's bodily needs, and teaches us exactly how to act in every situation. An appreciation of this leads one to love the Creator, Who guides us through life with such perfect care.

The Search for Harmony

Imagine how much more love and awe for Hashem we could attain if we found perfect synchronization between nature and the Torah. We would see that the magnificent patterns present in each are actually one and the same. Understanding how different aspects of nature are encoded in the Torah, and discovering how the lessons and patterns of the Torah are dramatically manifest in the natural world, are overwhelming and inspirational experiences.

Why should there be any synchronization between the two? Because to think that the Creator merely had a good day with His cosmic paintbrush when He created the world is a fallacy. The beautiful structure that surrounds us is the last stage of a process of creation that has its source in a far higher reality. It is a process which is defined by the Torah.

He looked into the Torah and created the world.

(Zohar, Terumah 161a)

The concept of the Torah as the blueprint of creation is familiar to many people. The precise meaning and mechanism of this, however, is rather complicated and tends to be less familiar. Let us examine this concept more closely and attain a better understanding of the nature of reality and the reality of nature.

Patterns in the Universe

For there is a high one who watches over him that is high; and there are yet higher ones over them.

(Koheles 5:8)

This verse describes the structure of reality. The universe we see is one of a long series of universes, stretching up to the highest spiritual realms.[8] There is a progressive unfolding of existence from Hashem's act of creation, with each successive layer being more removed from Him and thus from spirituality. We can imagine it as a "chain" of worlds, stretching between the Source of holiness and ourselves. This process culminates in the physical world that surrounds us. Being the furthest world from God, it has the lowest degree of sanctity and produces the greatest concealment of His presence.

We cannot grasp the nature of the worlds above us; we speak of them as "worlds" or "dimensions," but they do not have any form that we can comprehend. There is, however, a certain pattern present in each of these worlds. Each has the same structure, expressed in a form suited to that world. At every level the pattern is the same. In the words of the *Zohar*:

This world was made to reflect the world above it, and everything that exists above has its reflection below...

(*Zohar, Bereishis* 20a)

Thus, what we call a "hand" is only the physical manifestation of a hand. There are also varying degrees of spiritual "hands," which are metaphysical forces that are the equivalent of our hands. This is what is meant when the Torah speaks of the "hand of Hashem."[9]

Significantly, this self-similarity at different levels extends even within our world, where we've recently begun to notice the self-similarity present at different scales in nature. For example, a tiny section of fern leaf looks the same as a complete frond, which in turn looks the same as the whole leaf. The blood vessels within a person continually branch out, unfolding into smaller and smaller scales, yet retaining the same branching structure at each scale. This remarkable phenomenon has been given the term *fractal*. Fractal mathematics is the discovery by the secular world of the concept of *hishtalshelus*, the unfolding of a pattern from greater scales to lesser scales. (See Appendix A for a discussion of fractals.)

Note the two different variations of unfolding patterns. Within our world, the pattern is manifest identically at different scales, such as with leaves and blood vessels. Among the different worlds, the pattern is manifested in different forms, appropriate to each world.

This gives considerable insight into the nature of the ongoing process of creation. But we still do not have the key to understanding what this fractal pattern actually is. For that, we must look into the Torah.

Patterns in the Torah

The Torah itself travels through all the worlds, beginning from the highest spiritual source. It can thus be seen that at the source the Torah and the universe are one and the same. The Torah is therefore the code for all existence.[10]

Like the pattern of worlds, as the Torah unfolds through all the different dimensions it takes on the format most appropriate for each dimension. When it arrives in our world, it is manifest by talking about our world — mundane, everyday affairs, such as people and property. Yet this is only the outer garb of the Torah, the earthly manifestation of its essence.[11]

There is, however, an important difference between the nature of the worlds and of Torah. The worlds are progressively less holy in proportion to their distance from their source, ending in our world, which possesses the least sanctity. The Torah loses none of its sanctity in the process of its translation to different dimensions.[12]

Within the context of worlds, we identified two types of fractal unfolding. Among the different worlds, the same pattern is manifest differently. Within our dimension, the same pattern is repeated at different scales. The same is true of the Torah. Among the dimensions, it is the same code manifest differently. Within our dimension, the same pattern is repeated at different scales.

There is a five-stage pattern in the Torah which develops a process of growth, taking one from the extremes of egotism toward absolute dedication to Hashem and to mankind. This five-part structure exists at many different levels. It is found with the two tablets (each containing five commandments), with the five books of the Torah, within the individual books, and within the individual fifths of these books.[13] (See the Chart I illustrating part of this pattern at the end of the book.) The same pattern is repeated at different scales. The fractal nature of the world reflects the fractal nature of the Torah.

The Genetic Code

T he result of all this is that the Torah is a perfect description of all existence, because it is the root of existence. The Torah is not merely a body of information that accurately reports the state of reality. It is the very code from which reality has been formed. In the form of text on our bookshelves, it provides an understanding of the universe in which we live. Everything, from the orbits of planets to the shape of a fig leaf, from the dynamics of tornadoes to the markings on a leopard, has its source in the Torah. Everything we see is a physical manifestation of a higher reality.[14]

"So says Hashem: 'If I have not made a covenant with day and night and have not placed laws on heaven and earth...' " (Yirmeyahu 33:25). The covenant of the Torah is the basis for the laws of nature (Michtav MeEliyahu, vol. 1, p. 183).

Now, the concept of the universe being a physical manifestation of the Torah is a little hard to accept. After all, the revealed parts of the Torah can be contained in a few slim volumes — how could they be paralleled by all the intricacy of the universe?

Fortunately, there is a perfect parallel for this. Man is formed from amino acids, which are arranged into proteins by the genetic material known as DNA (an acronym for deoxyribonucleic acid). This genetic molecular code is relatively tiny compared to the vast richness of detail in the human being it produces. It works by condensing the information into an astonishingly compact form, something that astounded the scientists who discovered it. In the same way, the Torah is the genetic code for all of creation. It contains a much greater wealth of information than can be seen from simply reading the text. The Torah encodes data in myriads of different ways, from different groupings of its letters to the numerical values of different letters. (See Appendix B for an exploration into the parallels between Torah and DNA.)

In our generation, we lack the ability to decode the Torah properly. Shlomo HaMelech, with his great wisdom, knew how to unlock its secrets, and it was through this that he achieved such a great understanding of the natural world.[15] For the one who knows how to understand the Torah, it is all there. But the Sages did leave us some insights, which enable us to attain a greater understanding of the universe surrounding us.

"The information necessary to specify the design of all the species of organisms which have ever existed on the planet...could be held [by DNA] in a teaspoon and there would still be room left for all the information in every book ever written" (Denton, Evolution: A Theory in Crisis [Burnett Books, 1985], p. 334).

The Torah Universe

Understanding the harmony between Torah and nature will not only help us increase our love for the Creator and our awe of Him. We will also attain a greater understanding of our universe. Conversely, examination and contemplation of the universe will help us understand some of the more difficult parts of the Torah (as DNA did), and sensitivity to nature will help us become more sensitive to Torah. Understanding the synchronization between the two will help us lead more spiritually attuned lives in the midst of a physical world.

PART ONE

Concerning Time

CONCEPTS OF TIME

The Enigma of Time

Time is the framework within which changes and events occur. Rather than remain in a single state, the world is able to progress and develop or to regress and deteriorate. The total of all the changes that have occurred so far is what we call history.

The general view of time is that it progresses in a forward direction and that there is little more that can be said about it. The nature of time itself remains an enigma. Predicting social changes is considered an application of the social sciences and not connected with the inherent nature of time itself. Historical events which occurred when they did, did only that — *occur*. There was no force that made them happen at that precise moment, and had they happened a little earlier or a little later, it would not have made a difference.

According to this view of time, the calendar is a linear measuring tool drawn solely out of convenience. It simply helps create uniformity in planning activities for the future. Religious and national holidays are days on which everyone will simultaneously commemorate earlier events. When ten days were added to the year 1582, it was not universally accepted. For those who did accept it, the occurrence of the holidays for that year being less than 365 days after the previous year's holidays did not bother them. Since the Gregorian reform of 1752, when all calendars were synchronized, all the earlier alterations are considered irrelevant. People are not concerned that current calendar events do not occur a precise number of solar years after the original event took place.

Physical Cycles of Time

The Torah's portrayal of time is entirely different. It is based on the principle that everything in the physical world is a reflection of a higher spiritual reality. Thus, the spiritual realm has the same role vis-à-vis time as the physical world.

Time plays an innate, though not absolute, role in the development of the physical world. After spring comes summer, then autumn, then winter. After that, you can be sure that spring will arrive again. This repeating pattern determines when we sow seeds and when we harvest. Of course, it is not an absolute determinant; one could sow seeds in spring and harvest in winter. But this would not result in a particularly successful crop. There are specific times which are conducive to certain physical activities.

Conceptually, we could portray this repeating pattern as cyclical or circular. However, this pattern is not merely conceptual imagery; *it occurs because the physical reality is that way*. Planet Earth moves in an approximate circular path around the sun. It is this cyclical path, repeating itself annually, that produces the cycle of the seasons. (For a discussion of the precise geometric shape that describes the Earth's orbit and the flow of spiritual time, see Appendix C.)

The agricultural calendar, therefore, is not drawn arbitrarily. It is based on a repetitive and predictable set of circumstances. We do not sow seeds in autumn in *commemoration* of an event gone by. Rather, we sow seeds in autumn because this is the right time for this activity, because this autumn provides the correct environmental conditions in the same way as last year's autumn.

Spiritual Cycles of Time

The agricultural calendar is a precise reflection of the spiritual calendar. Different times of year provide conditions for different types of development. Certain times of the year are predisposed for renewal. Certain times of the year are conducive to joy. Certain times of the year are predestined for hardship. Again, these are not absolute determinants. One might not take the opportunity that spring provides to renew oneself. One might renew oneself at a different time. But the most successful growth will take place when it is in accordance with the spiritual seasons.

Just like time's physical development is of a cyclical structure, time's spiritual development is cyclical. Just as the seasons repeat themselves in a cycle, so do the seasons of spiritual "weather" repeat themselves.[1] The Earth's cyclical orbit models both physical time and spiritual time perfectly.

Our concept of time can also be seen in the very

word we use for time. *Zeman* is based on the root *zamein*, "prepared." We know in advance the nature of the future environments we will travel through — they have been prepared for us.[2] Purim has been prearranged to be a time of joy. Pesach has been prearranged to be a time of renewal. Again, the final course of events will depend on man's free will, but different points in time will be conducive to different choices and activities.

"To everything there is an appointed time and a place under the heavens: a time to be born and a time to die, a time to plant and a time to up-root that which has been planted...a time to weep and a time to rejoice..." (Koheles 2:3).

The same concept is clearly expressed in the Hebrew word for "year." *Shanah* comes from a root that can mean either "to repeat" or "to change," for every year contains the same basic elements of the previous year, but with new opportunities for growth.[3] This is the path of history, whereby each year allows for a new aspect of improvement, and this path will culminate when the world reaches a state of perfection.

Seasons of Life

This parallel between the physical and spiritual dimensions covers more than the conceptual flow of time alone, that it is cyclical. The various spiritual energies in effect at different times of the year are *directly manifest* in the natural cycle of the world at that time.[4] The seasons of weather and their effect on the world are a perfect reflection of the spiritual seasons. Plants, animals, and human beings all lead their lives in accordance with this pattern. The spiritual power of renewal that occurs in Nissan is physically manifest in the renewal of nature that occurs in spring. The spiritual time of hardship that takes place in Tamuz is reflected in the oppressive summer weather.

"...An appointed time for the world to be created, an appointed time for the generation of the Flood to be destroyed in water...an appointed time for our fathers to go down to Mitzrayim, and an appointed time for them to leave..." (Midrash Tanchuma, Eikev 9).

It is important to note that we are not talking about metaphors or symbolism. The aspects of nature that we will examine are not symbolic of spiritual matters — they are physical manifestations of them.

The seasons of life are twofold. There are nature's seasons of physical life in which plants and animals develop. And there are the Torah's seasons of spiritual life in which our minds and souls develop. We journey through seasons of the natural world and seasons of the soul. In this book, we will explore them both and discover how they are one at the root.

Rendezvous in Time

During the year we observe a variety of events in the calendar. These are not merely commemorations of earlier events. They are crucial points on the spiritual calendar to which we return each year. The festivals are called *chagim*, which is related to the root *chug*, "circle."[5] At each festival, we have come full circle, returning to the spiritual coordinates of the previous year.[6]

"In every generation a person is obligated to view himself as though he left Mitzrayim" (Pesach Haggadah).

The festivals are also called *mo'adim*. A *mo'ed* is a meeting, a rendezvous. On each of the three pilgrimage festivals (Pesach, Shavuos, Sukkos), we return to that special meeting place in time.[7]

> *Hashem said, "Let there be luminaries in the expanse of the skies...and let them be for signs and for mo'adim..."*
> (Bereishis 1:14)

The solar system does not serve simply to help us determine when to observe a festival. It denotes the arrival of the rendezvous, the very creation of the *mo'ed*. It does not tell us to observe Pesach because it was Pesach one year ago. It tells us that it is Pesach *now*. The sun and moon do not inform us of the date — they inform us of the situation. The luminaries are *for* the mo'adim.

Resolving the Enigma

The concept of cyclical time helps us understand some extremely puzzling sections in the Torah. Lot is described as serving matzos to his guests,[8] and Rashi explains that it was Pesach, though the Jewish people's descent to Mitzrayim was many years in the future. In another episode, when the Jewish people were about to leave Mitzrayim, they were instructed to observe the Festival of Matzos — before they had even thought about putting dough in the oven and taking it out before it could rise.[9]

These puzzling facts now make perfect sense. The festival of Pesach was in place long before the Jews went down to Mitzrayim. The observance of Pesach is based on the spiritual powers in force at that time of year. It is incorrect to say that we celebrate Pesach in the month of Nissan because we left Mitzrayim then; rather, we left Mitzrayim in Nissan because it was Pesach.[10] Nissan contains the energies that made it possible for us to leave Mitzrayim. The matzah is representative of certain metaphysical forces in effect at that time, as we shall discover. We are instructed to "guard the month of spring,"[11] which means we must arrange the calendar for the celebration of Pesach to occur during spring, for that is the time for Pesach.

The three major festivals are all linked by the Torah to the time in the agricultural year when they occur. Pesach is called the festival "in the appointed month of Spring,"[12] Shavuos is called the "Festival of Harvest,"[13] and Sukkos is called the "Festival of In-gathering."[14] The seasons are integral to the nature of the festivals.

Rendezvous in Space

> O Zion!...Through you the seasons were balanced on the true time line...
>
> *(Kinnos, "Tzion Kechi")*

The pattern of seasons in the calendar that we shall describe does not hold true, of course, for the whole world. It is designed for Eretz Yisrael (though it will also function to a certain extent for countries with the same latitude and general climate[15]). The reason for this is simple: Eretz Yisrael is the designated place for the performance of Hashem's commandments. For those of us who do not live in Eretz Yisrael and lack the sensory input of the physical seasons to enhance our un-derstanding of the calendar, it is all the more important to apply our minds to studying the pattern of the year.

"O Zion!...The birth of the new moon [fixes the month] according to your longitude, its visibility was measured according to your latitude, and through it your secrets were revealed" (Kinnos, "Tzion Kechi").

The seasons of Eretz Yisrael provide the perfect set-ting for the *mo'adim*. Yet Eretz Yisrael is essential to a *mo'ed* in another way, too. We already described the *mo'adim* as rendezvous with Hashem in time. But at each *mo'ed*, we also rendezvoused with Hashem in space. Pesach, Shavuos, and Sukkos brought us to Yerushalayim and the Beis HaMikdash. The Beis HaMikdash was the conduit between our world and the higher spiritual worlds. (This concept will be discussed further in "Cheshvan.") When we gathered at the Beis HaMikdash, there was a rendezvous in space, time, and spirituality.

The Zodiac

The Divine forces that govern this world filter down through the chain of worlds from Hashem to us. The world immediately preceding ours is the realm manifest by the constellations. The zodiac is called *mazal* in Hebrew, which is based on the word *nozel*, "flow." The constellations are conduits for the flow of spiritual energy from higher to lower dimensions.[16] It is unfortunate that *mazal* is sometimes translated as "luck," for it is the very opposite of luck! *Mazal* is not random; it is a system of predetermination.

When we examine the situation of the Jewish people vis-à-vis *mazalos*, however, matters become somewhat complex. When Avraham protested to Hashem that astrology predicted he would have only one son,[17] Yishmael, Hashem replied, "Release yourself from the influence of the stars, for Israel is beyond the constellations."[18] It would seem from here that the zodiac has no bearing on us. The Gemara says this quite succinctly:

Yisrael has no *mazal*.

(*Shabbos* 156a)

The answer is that the constellations do not absolutely determine our situation. They form a set of tools which can either manipulate us or be manipulated by us. While they do present a predetermination, we can, if we are of adequate spiritual standing, manipulate the zodiac to our benefit.[19]

Thus, when Hashem granted another son to Avraham, He did not simply disregard the *mazalos*. Hashem told Avraham: "Your ruling planet is Tzedek (Jupiter), which appears in the west and indicates that you are not able to have any more children. I shall move it to the east, so that you will father another child..."[20]

In the course of our journey through the year, we shall often note how the forces present in the month are expressed by the zodiac sign for that month. These are not forces controlling us; rather, they represent the spiritual tools we can utilize during that month.

SELECTING A CALENDAR

The Planetary Calendar

What is a year? Some cultures follow the solar year, which is defined as the time it takes for Earth to complete one revolution around the sun. This system entirely negates the significance of the months, considering them merely convenient divisions of the year. Others follow the lunar year, comprised of twelve lunar months, a lunar month being the time it takes the moon to complete one cycle of waxing and waning. However, since twelve lunar months are only 354 days, and the solar year is 365 days, the seasons (which are solar-based) always occur at a different time of year on the lunar calendar. If we were to follow the lunar calendar alone, Pesach would often occur in winter.

The Torah tells us to keep track of both the sun and the moon. We measure lunar months and count twelve of these to produce a year. This is a total of 354 days and only approximately equals one revolution of the Earth around the sun. The Torah, therefore, tells us that some years we must add a thirteenth month to keep our lunar calendar aligned with the sun and the seasons. Let us explore the significance of this calendar system.

Lunar Months

"He made the moon for the festivals..." (Tehillim 104:19).

The moon is the focal point of our calendar. The first commandment that was given to us as a nation was the mitzvah of sanctifying the new moon and creating a calendar around it.[1] The Jewish people are compared to the moon, in a variety of ways. Unlike the sun, which produces its own light, the moon reflects light. It possesses no light of its own. In the same way, the Jewish people acknowledge that they do not possess an innate right of existence.[2] We receive our life from the Creator (light is often used as a metaphor for life force). Other peoples — who do not acknowledge that their existence stems from a higher source, but believe that they themselves are responsible for their existence — manifest this belief by basing their calendar on the sun, which produces its own light.[3]

Another significant aspect of the moon is that it appears to grow and shrink in the course of a month. It changes constantly, from one night to the next. The sun, on the other hand, is fixed, staying the same size whenever we look at it.

The moon always reflects the same amount of sunlight, but that part of the moon is not always visible to us. Similarly, we are always under Hashem's care, but sometimes Hashem "hides His face," which is called "hester panim" (Kenaf Renanim on Perek Shirah, "Song of the Moon").

This parallels the difference between the Jewish people and the other nations of the world. The latter are governed by a strict set of rules — the rules of history decreed by Hashem. They follow the set pattern of social course. The Jewish people, however, defy explanation by historians. We rise and fall like no other people. We have, in the course of our history, changed from being a battered slave tribe to being one of the mightiest peoples of the time. We have fallen unpredictably, at times when our people were trying to emulate our neighbors in a way that the historians' rules predicted would boost chances for survival. Yet, unlike any other people dispersed so far and wide, we remain. We have the power of *hischadshus*, renewal and rebirth. A month is called "*chodesh*," from the same root. The monthly renewal of the moon is the manifestation of the power we possess.[4]

The amount of light reflected by the moon depends on how much of the visible part of the moon faces the sun. In the same way, Hashem is an illuminating Force for us only to the extent that we are facing Him, that we turn to His Torah. When we turn away from Him, we no longer absorb His Light; we are open to attack and we fade away. But when we return to Him in repentance, we are able to renew ourselves and receive His Light once more, just as the moon renews itself and receives the sun's light once again.[5]

"To the moon He said that it should renew itself as a crown of splendor for those borne [by Him] from the womb, those who are destined to renew themselves like it..." (Kiddush Levanah).

"May it be Your will, Hashem...to fill the deficiency of the moon that there be no diminution in it. May the light of the moon be like the light of the sun and like the light of the seven days of Creation, as it was before it was diminished..." (Kiddush Levanah). (See Shem MiShmuel, Rosh Chodesh Nissan 5673, for a fascinating explanation of the process involved.)

Solar Years

Adding a month to the lunar calendar to keep it aligned with the solar year is needed to ensure that we celebrate Pesach in spring and Sukkos in the fall. But the reason for leap years goes far deeper.

> Rabbi Nachman said: "This is a good sign; Eisav counts according to the sun, which is large. And just as the sun shines during the day but not at night, so too does Eisav have a portion in this world but not in the next. Yaakov counts according to the moon, which is small, and just as the moon shines both at night and during the day, so too does Yaakov have a portion both in this world and in the World to Come..."
>
> *(Bereishis Rabbah 6:3)*

The sun represents strength and might. Blazing in all its glory, it sets the stage for material development as the symbol of this material world. But its reign is restricted to the day alone. The moon, on the other hand, presents its modest light, light which allows only for spiritual development. Yet the moon can be seen during the day as well as during the night, a quietly visible presence.

This relates to two divergent paths that lie before us. There is the path of spiritual aspirations, taken by Yaakov and his descendants, the Jewish people. And there is the path of material aspirations, taken by Eisav and his progeny, the culture of ancient Rome and Western civilization.

Eisav "lives by the sword"[6] and for the purpose of material wealth and power. His descendants strive for dominion in this world and engage in the construction of mighty empires. But, like the sun, which vanishes at the onset of night, Eisav's reign is limited. Eventually his power will crumble, and he will fade to nothingness.

Yaakov takes a very different path. He chooses to forego material wealth and allows Eisav to take a dominant role. It is spirituality that interests Yaakov, not material power. Like the moon during the day, he is thereby resigned to a modest, background presence. He pales into insignificance next to the material glory of Eisav. But ultimately he will triumph:

> All the time that the larger luminary shines, the light of the smaller cannot be seen. When the larger luminary sets, the light of the smaller can be seen. So, too, as long as the light of Eisav shines, the light of Yaakov cannot be seen. But when the light of Eisav sets, the light of Yaakov blazes forth...
>
> (Ibid.)

By striving for the values of spirituality and eternity we will prove ultimately victorious over Eisav. At the end of the day, it is the moon that triumphs over the sun. In terms of measuring years, this means that while our concept is essentially lunar, we create leap years to catch up eventually with the solar year. The controversy between the spiritual mission and the material mission is ultimately reconciled. In the short term, we lag behind, but eventually we triumph.[7] (This concept is explored further in "Adar.")

DIVIDING
THE CALENDAR

Years: Theory and Practice

Now that we understand the type of calendar we use, let us explore the way in which we divide the calendar. First, we must study the month in which the year begins. That shouldn't be too difficult — we'll simply see in which month the world was created.

> Rabbi Eliezer states: "The world was created in Tishrei..." Rabbi Yehoshua states: "The world was created in Nissan..."
>
> (*Rosh HaShanah* 10b)

Can such a basic historical fact really be the subject of dispute? *Tosafos*[1] explain that both statements are "the words of the Living God"; in Tishrei God decided to create the world, but He did not actually create it until Nissan. What caused this apparent hesitation?

> He originally thought to create the world with the attribute of *din* [judgment], but He saw that the world could not exist this way, so He brought forward the attribute of

rachamim [mercy] and combined it with *din.*

(Rashi on Bereishis 1:1)

Obviously Hashem did not change His mind or make a mistake in the design stage. The full depth of meaning of these words is beyond us, but at a simple level we can see that there are two conceptual beginnings to the world. The first beginning, in *thought,* utilizes the attribute of *din,* strict judgment. When the laws of the universe were conceived, they were designed to be absolute, following strict rules. The second beginning, in *deed*, utilizes the attribute of *rachamim.* A degree of flexibility was applied in a way that allows for deviations from the order of nature.

The first beginning, in Tishrei, is Rosh HaShanah for the whole world. It is the day when the world was designed with the rules Hashem uses to govern it. The second beginning, in Nissan, is a new beginning for the Jewish people. In that month, we left the exile of Mitzrayim in a supernatural manner. Thus, Nissan began a new order for us, an order of *rachamim,* the possibility of defying the natural order.[2]

We acknowledge, therefore, that the first of Tishrei is the New Year for the world as a whole; we count the years since the creation of the world from that date. But we observe the first of Nissan as the New Year for our process of spiritual development. It was in Nissan that we experienced the all-time (so far) maximum renewal of the Exodus. It is for this month that we were given the mitzvah of *"hachodesh hazeh lachem...* — this month shall be for you the head of the months,"[3] the mitzvah of establishing the lunar calendar. As we have seen, the moon represents the concept of renewal and change, the ability to go against the regular laws of the world. Therefore, on the day we began the process of renewal we start counting the ever important lunar months.

A summary of this is found in the Mishnah:

> The first of Nissan is the New Year for festivals [i.e., the process of spiritual development]... The first of Tishrei is the New Year for years [i.e., the general cycle of the world]...
>
> (*Rosh HaShanah* 2a)

We also see that these two beginnings, that of *din* and that of *rachamim*, are paralleled by the crops. Tishrei, when the crop is harvested and brought into the storehouses, is the beginning of the year in *din*. *Din* means judging a situation according to its merits as they stand at the moment. Just as the crops are assessed according to how they turn out, so too, the world is judged according to its actual progress.

Nissan, on the other hand, is the beginning of the year in *rachamim*. It is the season in which the crops are only half-developed, and it is still unclear as to how they will turn out. *Rachamim* means taking into account the possibility of future improvement.[4] Just as in Nissan we cannot say with finality what the final crop will look like, so too does Hashem take into account the possibility of future progress in His judgment of us.

Years: Physical and Spiritual

The two beginnings to the year can be seen as counting two different types of year.[5] One type correlates to this physical world. It begins in the darkness of fall (Tishrei), and although it rises through the light of summer, it ends again in the fall. That is the story of man's physical existence. Man is born from dust, and, no matter how spectacular a life he may lead, he returns to dust. The empires of Egypt and Rome may have risen to dizzying levels of material wealth and power, but nothing remains of them now. Nothing in the physical world lasts. Everything begins in darkness and ends in darkness.

The other type of year begins with the light of spring (Nissan), and even though it passes through the harshness of winter, it concludes with the brightness of spring. That year relates to our spiritual existence as Jews. Our beginning is in the light of Gan Eden, and, although we pass through times of darkness in the exiles of this world, we end once again in the light of the World to Come.[6] Thus, Tishrei in the fall is the beginning of the earthly year, and Nissan in spring is the beginning of the spiritual year.

Following the same pattern, there is a dual day. One type of day, which the Torah prescribes for mankind in general, begins at night, and although it passes through the light of day, it ends the next night. This day follows the dust-to-dust pattern of the physical world. But there is another, spiritual type of day, which was used in the calendar of the Beis HaMikdash. It began in the morning, and although it passed through the darkness of night, it ended in the light of the morning.[7] Such is the pattern of spirituality.

"And you shall study [the Torah] day and night" (Yehoshua 1:8). The order of this verse shows us that for the purpose of the daily blessing on the Torah, the day includes the following night; a spiritual task such as this follows the pattern of the spiritual day (Dover Shalom on birkas haTorah in Siddur Otzar HaTefillos).

Four Quarters

The year is divided into four quarters called "*tekufos.*" The term *tekufos* also refers to the special days that begin each of these quarters.

These are based on the relative positions of the sun and the Earth. At the spring and autumnal equinoxes (*tekufas Nissan* and *tekufas Tishrei*), the Earth is angled with the sun in such a way that the day and night are of equal length. The summer solstice (*tekufas Tamuz*) is the longest day and shortest night; the winter solstice (*tekufas Teves*) is the longest night and shortest day. These two categories, the equinoxes and the solstices, represent two distinct situations in the year.

Judaism is a religion of balance. In virtually all areas of character development, the middle path is encouraged and extremes are to be shunned.[8] Thus, one should be happy, but not frivolous; confident, but not haughty. In other aspects, too, we see balance: there are days when it is a mitzvah to eat and days when we are required to fast. Eating itself should be done in moderation. Even in the Land of Israel we find a gentle balance of grassy plains and wooded hills; the mountains' altitudes are hardly record-breaking, nor is the desert particularly harsh.[9]

In the same way, the most favorable times of year for us are Nissan in the spring and Tishrei in the autumn. Those times, when the weather is temperate, reflect a favorable situation for the Jewish people, and it is then that we celebrate Pesach and Sukkos.[10] On the other hand, the hot summer months of Tamuz and Av are an extreme point in the year. The temperature signifies the Destruction, a theme of that period, when we observe the fasts of the Seventeenth of Tamuz and Tishah B'Av. Similarly, the cold month of Teves demonstrates an unfavorable period, and it is then that we observe the fast of the Tenth of Teves. Thus, the Torah's preference of moderateness over extremes is expressed in the synchronization of the spiritual and physical seasons.[11]

Six Seasons

Contrary to popular conception, there are six seasons in the year, not four. When Noach left the ark, Hashem promised that He would not destroy the world again. He assured Noach that the world would continually function according to a fixed cycle:

עד כל ימי הארץ זרע וקציר וקר וחם וקיץ וחרף ויום ולילה לא ישבתו.

For the rest of the days of the earth, fall seedtime and spring harvest, late winter and late summer, high summer and deep winter, and day and night shall not cease.

(Bereishis 8:22)

Six seasons are defined here:[12]

1. קציר (*katzir*), "spring harvest" (literally, "harvest"). This consists of the months of Nissan and Iyar, which begin the harvest period.[13] It contains the festival of Pesach and most of *sefiras ha'omer*, the count-up from the barley offering to Shavuos.

2. קיץ (*kayitz*), "high summer." This consists of the months of Sivan, which contains the festival of Shavuos, and Tamuz, in which we fast on the seventeenth of the month. The summer solstice, when the sun is at its maximum strength, occurs during this season.

3. חם (*chom*), "late summer" (literally, "heat"). This is the time when the heat of the summer accumulates to its greatest intensity.[14] This hottest season occurs later than the summer

"The end of summer is the harshest part of summer..." (Yoma 29a).

solstice, due to the insulating effect of the Earth's surface, which takes a long time to recover from the cold of winter. Late summer consists of the months of Av and Elul. The Ninth of Av is when the destruction of both the first and second Batei Mikdash occurred.

4. זרע (*zera*), "fall seedtime" (literally, "seedtime"). This is when the crops are sown. This season contains Tishrei (which actually means "fall") and Cheshvan. Tishrei contains Rosh HaShanah, Yom Kippur, and Sukkos.

5. חרף (*choref*), "deep winter." This season consists of the months of Kislev, in which we celebrate Chanukah, and Teves, on the tenth of which we fast. The winter solstice occurs in this season.

6. קר (*kor*), "late winter" (literally, "cold"). This season is furthest from the warmth of the summer months — the increase in the sun's power is counteracted by the insulating effect of the Earth's surface. It consists of the final months of the year: Shevat, containing the New Year for trees, and Adar, the month of Purim.

Twelve Months

The year is divided into twelve lunar months (thirteen in a leap year), starting from Nissan, as explained. In the Torah, these months have no names; they are simply counted from Nissan, with Nissan being called *chodesh harishon*, "the first month," Iyar, *hasheini*, "the second," and so on. This is due to the central importance of Nissan, the month of redemption.

The Torah tells us that Nissan shall be "the head of the months";[15] included in this is the requirement to count the months in such a way that this is made clear.[16] Thus, by calling Iyar the second month we are fulfilling the commandment of making Nissan the first month, and we are commemorating the importance of the Exodus.

Why, then, are we allowed to use the names *Nissan, Iyar,* and so on? These names are traced back to Bavel,[17] though some say they existed since Sinai.[18] The rationale for using these names is that since we have merited several redemptions from exile since the Exodus, it is no longer essential to date the months from that redemption.[19] This is alluded to by the prophet Yirmeyahu:

> *"Therefore, behold, days are coming," says Hashem, "when it shall no longer be said, 'As Hashem lives, Who brought the children of Yisrael out of Mitzrayim,' but 'As Hashem lives, Who brought up the children of Yisrael out of the northern land...' "*
> (Yirmeyahu 16:14–15)

Still, one may wonder what the actual motivation was for using the Babylonian names. Even more bizarre, some of these names are those of pagan deities, such as Tamuz.[20] Why are these names used?

The answer is that the exodus from Bavel was under great risk of misinterpretation. The nation as a whole was likely to see it as a complete, possibly final, redemption. But the Sages knew that such was not the case. It was only a concession to the spiritually weak state of the people. Hashem allowed the temporary rebuilding of the Beis HaMikdash to spiritually strengthen the Jewish people for the many years of exile that lay ahead. The Sages therefore thought it essential to stress from the outset that the redemption from Bavel was in-

Many Sages used Aramaic names for the same reason; nowadays, however, it is more important to use Jewish names to prevent assimilation (Emes L'Yaakov on Shemos 12:2, in footnote).

complete; one way of making this point was to use the months' Babylonian names.[21]

The Unique Week

The week is strikingly different from the year, month, or day. These are all based on planetary motion, but no such basis seems to exist for the week. Furthermore, there is no apparent role of this period of time in nature.[22] Yet the week, as represented by Shabbos (we shall discover the reason for this later), should surely be the most important time period to be represented in nature. As we say in Kiddush, the whole point of Shabbos and the structure of the week is to attest to the original week of the Creation:

> Blessed are You, Hashem...Who bequeathed to us His holy Shabbos with love and favor, as a remembrance of Creation.
>
> (Kiddush of Shabbos eve)

Perhaps we should explore the number seven. After all, the week is significant in that it consists of seven days. But there does not seem to be any fundamental relevance to the number seven in nature. So where is the relevance of the week in the natural world?

The answer lies in a fuller understanding of the week and the role of Shabbos as a testimony to Hashem's creation of the world. Let us first pose some simple, yet fundamental, questions about Shabbos.

If Shabbos is testimony to the fact that Hashem created the world, wouldn't it make more sense to celebrate it on Sunday, the day when He *began* creating? After all, surely the first day, when God created ex nihilo, "something from nothing," is of greater significance than the later stages, which were only transformations of that which had already been created. Furthermore, if we are testifying to His creation, we should do so by creating something ourselves. Instead, we abstain from work — the opposite of creation.

These perplexing difficulties are resolved when one looks at what Shabbos is really meant to signify. Granted, it attests to Hashem's creation of the world, but not in the ex nihilo aspect. It testifies to Hashem having created the world *meaningfully,* for a purpose. If we were just celebrating the creation of the world from nothing, it would indeed make more sense to do so on Sunday. But we are celebrating something more than that. It is the purpose of Creation that is of real significance; it is the goal for which the world was created that we celebrate.

"You sanctified the seventh day for Your Name, the purpose of the heavens and earth..." (mussaf prayer on Shabbos).

Which creature was created to achieve this goal? Man. It was only after the creation of man that we find that

> God saw all *that He had made, and behold, it was* very good...
> (Bereishis 1:31)

Hashem saw "all," the entire world, completed with the creation of man. With the creation of man, the world was ready to reach its goal. What is this goal? For man to draw close to His Creator, through learning Torah and performing mitzvos.

Every week, we testify to the purpose of Creation. We spend one day free from any creative acts in the physical sphere. We spend one day involved in the realm of purpose. We spend one day dedicated to Torah and spirituality.

This explains why the week is represented by Shabbos. Each day is significant only in terms of it being part of a process, the goal of which is reached on

Shabbos. We do not name our days after Norse deities. Instead, we have "the first day to Shabbos," "the second day to Shabbos," and so on. Each day is identified by its role as part of the week, whose purpose is Shabbos. The very naming of the days is a fulfillment of "Remember the Shabbos day to sanctify it."[23]

Shabbos is not an inherent part of nature. It is something that Hashem and the Jewish people *designate*. Hashem created the world for a purpose; we actualize that purpose. Between us, we designate this day as a special day.

Now we can understand why the week and Shabbos are not found in nature. They are to be *pronounced* upon nature, to be superimposed upon nature's calendar, thereby designating and sanctifying the world as purposeful. This is done only by the Jewish people, the central players in the purpose of creation. In the Shabbos prayers, we say, "Hashem our God did not give [Shabbos] to the nations of the lands...only to the Jews..." Shabbos is not part of nature; therefore the non-Jews have no claim to it. Shabbos is the demonstration that the natural world was created for a purpose, by the people who are to fulfill that purpose.

Taking another look at the number seven, perhaps we can find a small but significant occurrence of it in nature. There are seven colors in a rainbow (red, orange, yellow, green, blue, indigo, violet). The rainbow was not designed as an inherent part of nature. It was added after the Flood as a message from Hashem that He owns the world and will allow its continued existence. Again, the number seven is not part of the natural world; it is Hashem's mark of the natural world as being His purposeful creation.

"The wedding of a virgin should be held on the fourth day of the week and the marriage consummated on the fifth, for on the fifth day of Creation the fish were blessed that they be fruitful. The wedding of a widow should be on the fifth day and the marriage consummated on the sixth day, for on the sixth day of Creation man was blessed that he be fruitful and multiply" (Kesubos 5a). The days of the week each contain unique spiritual powers.

Days of All Sizes

*For the rest of the days of the earth, seedtime and harvest, cold
and heat, summer and winter...shall not cease.*

(Bereishis 8:22)

A precise reading of this verse indicates that each
"day of the earth" contains all of these seasons. Although the term *day* usually refers to a time span of
twenty-four hours, here we see it used to describe a
whole year.[24]

A day is a microcosm of a year; they share the
same features. At the physical level, this is obvious.
Both contain a light, warm section (daytime; summer),
and a cold, dark section (nighttime; winter). Another
clear parallel is that both days and years flow in cycles
of seven, with every seventh being a rest period. Every
seventh day is Shabbos; every seventh year is *shemittah*
(the sabbatical year). The Torah even refers to
shemittah as "Shabbos."[25] Another parallel, as we discussed, is that both days and years have a dual nature,
with one beginning and end for the "regular" day and
year and another beginning and end for the "holy" day
and year.

The forces present during the different times of
year are also present at the equivalent time of the day, at
a reduced level. For example, the power of renewal occurs during the year at Nissan and during the day in the
morning. Some aspects of the pattern are more difficult
to discern in the smaller duration of the day. Nevertheless, a careful study of the description of the year will
yield many insights into the flow of the day.

*For a thousand years are in Your eyes as one fleeting day of yes-
terday...*

(Tehillim 90:4)

In addition to the twenty-four-hour day and the twelve-month "day," there is also the thousand-year "day." This day, however, is used only in Hashem's calendar. Again, this occurs in a cycle of seven. The history of our world will last for a total of six such days — that is, six thousand years — after which it will be followed by "Shabbos," the World to Come.[26]

Again, we see identical patterns repeated on different scales — another example of the fractal nature of the Torah universe.

PATTERNS AND ELEMENTS

Micro and Macro Perspectives

In the twentieth century, when there is a trend toward specialization, we tend to focus on small aspects of matters, ignoring the bigger picture. As we explore the different elements of the year, we must remember that none of these are isolated points. They are all parts of bigger patterns (which are in turn subsumed into even bigger patterns, and so on, on a fractal basis).

In these pages we will explore three of the patterns that are manifest throughout the year. Since it is worthwhile to have these patterns in mind before we analyze the year in depth, we will present a brief outline of these patterns in this chapter; then, as we travel through the year, we will examine the details.

Relationships

The most important aspect of the seasons is the rain cycle, since the physical sustenance of the world depends on it. And since everything physical reflects the spiritual, the rain cycle is therefore of profound spiritual significance.

The relationship between Hashem and the Jewish people is often expressed as a male-female relationship. The Torah speaks of Hashem in the masculine gender. Obviously Hashem is not a man, but in terms of our relationship with Him, Hashem has the male role. We human beings on Earth, in turn, have a female role, which is why the word for this world, *eretz*, is in the feminine gender. The book of Shir HaShirim, which appears to be a love song between a man and woman, is actually a song between Hashem and the Jewish people.

The terms *male* and *female* are used to describe the roles of giver and receiver, as is also clear on a biological level. Hashem, in the male role, provides materials, forces, and abilities. The female role of the Jewish people is to receive these things and develop them. Hashem provides us with life, and it is our task to take it and use it correctly. Hashem gives us a world, and we try to perfect it. Hashem presents us with the Torah, and we are bidden to expound on it and form insights.

"From when do we pronounce the blessing on rain? From when the groom [the rain] goes out to meet the bride [the earth]" (Ta'anis 6b).

An identical relationship exists between the skies and the land. The skies provide rain, which fertilize the land and enable it to "give birth" to crops and flowers. The Gemara succinctly expresses this concept:

> Rabbi Yehudah said: "The rain is the husband of the land..."
>
> (*Ta'anis* 6b)

The relationship of the rain to the land is therefore the physical manifestation of the relationship between Hashem and the Jewish people.[1]

Heaven and Earth

Although rain can be the medium of relationship between Hashem and the Jewish people, it should be noted that not all rains are equal:

Rabbi Yochanan said: "The clouds are formed from the upper waters, as it says, *...with the clouds of the Heaven* (Daniel 7:13)." Reish Lakish said: "The clouds are formed from the lower waters, as it says, *He causes vapor to ascend from the ends of the earth* (Tehillim 135:7)."

(*Bereishis Rabbah* 13:11)[2]

Rabbi Yochanan and Reish Lakish are not discussing where the molecules of H_2O in the clouds actually come from — clearly, they come from evaporated water. They are discussing where the *essence* of the rain comes from — whether it is a spiritual gift from the heavens or merely a physical process. The Vilna Gaon[3] explains that there is no argument here: "One refers to when Yisrael are fulfilling the will of Hashem, and the other refers to when Yisrael are not fulfilling the will of Hashem."[4] If man performs the will of his Creator, the rain that falls is of spiritual essence. Man has the capacity to join Heaven and earth:

And He blew into his nostrils the breath of life — He made man from both upper and lower: his body from the lower elements, and his soul from the upper elements. For on the first day He created the heavens and the earth, on the second day He created the firmament for the upper elements, on the third day He revealed the dry land for the lower elements, on the fourth day He created the luminaries for the upper elements, and on the fifth day He caused the waters to swarm [with life] for the lower elements; on the sixth day, therefore, He was required to create something from both the upper and lower elements, so that there should not be any jealousy in the acts of creation, that one should have an extra day of creation.

(*Rashi*, on Bereishis 2:7)[5]

The rain does not fall unless the sins of Yisrael have been forgiven, as it says (Tehillim 85:2–3), "Hashem, You have been favorable to Your land, You have brought back the captives of Yaakov, You have forgiven the sin of Your people, You have pardoned their sins, selah!" (Ta'anis 7b).

The two names for rain, matar and geshem, refer to the spiritual and physical varieties of rain (Malbim on Bereishis 1:6; see also Malbim on Bereishis 2:5).

The supernatural essence of rain is expressed in its nondeterministic character, making long-term rainfall predictions impossible for science (see the section "The Power of Life" in "Cheshvan").

Man can earn a rainfall that is purely an expression of Hashem's beneficence. Its spiritual essence will be expressed in its abundant quantities[6] and its falling at the most useful times.[7] But if man does not perform the will of Hashem, then the link between heaven and earth is not created, and the rain that falls will be solely of a physical nature. It will consist only of evaporated water, with no higher spiritual essence. Such was the situation before man was created:

> ...Hashem, God, had not caused it to rain on the land, and there was no man to work the ground. And a mist would go up from the land and water the face of the ground.
>
> (Bereishis 2:5–6)[8]

Life Cycles

The relationship between Hashem and the Jewish people, which is manifest by the rain, progresses in an annual cycle, one which is a microcosm of a lifetime. Nissan, spring, is the stage of birth, as shown by the renewal of the natural world. In Iyar we develop, and in Sivan we reach maturity, along with the crops. In Av and Elul we prepare to relate to Hashem. Tishrei, the advent of the rainy season, is the realization of this relationship. In the winter, while the seeds germinate underground, we go through a process of development, preparing for the rebirth of spring and the next cycle of growth. This is the general pattern of the seasons which we will explore in depth.

This relationship, unique to the Jewish people, is a special feature of Eretz Yisrael:

> For the land which you are entering to possess is not like the land of Egypt, which you left, where you sow your seeds and water it

"From the day the Beis HaMikdash was destroyed, the rain has not fallen from the good storehouse, as it is written, '[If you listen to the voice of Hashem...] Hashem shall open for you His good storehouse [...to give the rain to your land]' (Devarim 28:12). When Yisrael fulfill the will of Hashem and are settled in their land, the rain falls from the good storehouse; when Yisrael do not fulfill the will of Hashem and are not settled in their land, the rain does not fall from the good storehouse" (Bava Basra 25b; cf. Parashas Derachim, derush 21).

by walking [to bring water from the Nile], like a vegetable gar-
den [which requires supplementary irrigation]. The land into
which you are passing to inherit is a land of hills and valleys,
which drinks water from the rain of the heavens, a land which
Hashem your God constantly cares for...[9]

(Devarim 11:10–12)

"Hashem Himself waters Eretz Yisrael, and the rest of the world is watered through an intermediary [shaliach], as it says (Iyov 5:10), 'He gives rain on the face of the land [Eretz Yisrael] and sends [sholei'ach] water on the face of the fields' " (Ta'anis 10a).

Mirror Image

As long as the earth lasts, seedtime and harvest, late summer
and late winter, deep winter and high summer...shall not cease.

(Bereishis 8:22)

The structure of this verse is interesting. It does not present the seasons in their order of occurrence. Rather, each season is presented together with the season that occurs furthest away from it. If we visualize the year as a circle, then each season is paired with the one opposite.

The significance of this pattern is that each part of the year contains elements which complement the elements in its opposite. To note but a few examples: Nissan is the beginning of the year for the order of *chesed* (kindness), and Tishrei begins the new year for *din* (judgment). Shavuos, in Sivan, celebrates the giving of the Written Torah, while Chanukah, in Kislev, marks the victory of the Oral Torah over Greek philosophy. In Elul, our *teshuvah* is motivated by awe of Hashem, while in Adar it is inspired by our love of Him. (These and other instances of this phenomenon are discussed in their respective places of occurrence. A chart, illustrating these patterns, is at the back of the book in the section "Time Cycles.")

Four Non-kosher Evils

When Hashem created the world, He built into it four imperfections. These have been manifest during history as the four kingdoms under which we have been exiled.[10] In chronological order, these are Bavel (Babylon), Paras and Madai (Persia and Media), Yavan (Greece), and Edom (Eisav; Rome; Western civilization). The forces these kingdoms represent are active at different times of the year.[11]

"There is no man without his hour..." (Avos 4:3). All the more so concerning a nation.

These four forces of evil are manifest in other ways. Two of these patterns are of concern to us here, in which the kingdoms are paralleled by different sets of animals, as explained in the Midrash.[12]

The Torah tells us that for an animal to be kosher for consumption, it must ruminate (chew its cud) and have split hooves. There are four animals, says the Torah, which possess only one of these two features and are therefore non-kosher. (The identification of these creatures is discussed at length in the endnotes.)

1. The *gamal* (camel) chews its cud but does not have a true hoof.[13] This parallels Bavel and shall be discussed in the section on Av, the month in which Bavel destroyed the first Beis HaMikdash.

2. *Shafan*, which seems to refer to the hyrax, is a small creature resembling a guinea pig.[14] It is described as an animal which chews its cud but does not have a true hoof. It parallels Persia and Media, which are discussed in the section on Adar, the month of Purim. The hyrax is also discussed in the section on Rosh Chodesh.

3. *Arneves*, which is probably the hare, is described as chewing its cud but not possessing a hoof.[15] It is paralleled by Greece and is discussed in the section on Kislev, in which we celebrate Chanukah, the victory over Greece.

4. *Chazir* (pig) has split hooves but does not ruminate and parallels Edom. In other places it is sometimes referred to as *chazir miya'ar* (forest pig), known today as the wild boar. It is discussed both in the section on Av, the month in which Rome destroyed the Second Beis Ha-Mikdash, and in the section on Adar.

Four Wild Evils

Daniel spoke and said, "I saw in my vision by night, and behold, the four winds of the heaven stirred up the great sea. Four great beasts came up from the sea, each different from the other..."
(Daniel 7:2–3)

The four terrifying creatures which the prophet Daniel saw in his vision also parallel the four kingdoms:

1. "The first was like a lion, and it had the wings of a *nesher* [vulture or eagle[16]]." The parallels between the first kingdom, Bavel, and the lion shall be explored in the section on Av.

2. "And behold, another beast, a second one, similar to a bear[17]..." This represents Persia (and Media) and is discussed in the section on Adar.

3. "Afterwards I beheld, and there was another, similar to a leopard..." The leopard parallels

Yavan and is discussed in the section on Kislev.

4. "After this I saw in my visions of the night a fourth beast, terrible and terrifying and extremely powerful, with great iron teeth..." This creature is not based on an animal, but is a new creation, a metal-mouthed monster which represents the power of Edom.

PART TWO

Within Time

ROSH CHODESH

Master of Creation

Rabbi Yochanan said: "One who blesses the new moon is regarded as though he has greeted the *Shechinah* [Divine Presence]..."

(Sanhedrin 42a)

When the new moon appears, we recite *Kiddush Levanah*, the sanctification of the new moon. The accolade the above *gemara* grants to this blessing is quite remarkable. Why is this prayer so significant?

One of the threats that faced Judaism throughout history was the false ideology of a static universe. Before the advent of the big-bang theory, the viewpoint presented by atheists was the steady-state theory, that the universe had always existed. There was no beginning to the universe and no creation. Everything has always existed the way it exists now; planet Earth has always traveled around the sun as it does now. There was no place for a Creator in their ideology. The masses accepted this theory, for they saw the planets following an organized, set pattern — why suggest it was ever any different?

But when we contemplate the moon, we begin to think differently. The waxing and waning of the moon

"If Yisrael merited to receive the presence of their Father in heaven only once a month, it would be enough" (Sanhedrin 42a, recited in Kiddush Levanah).

is a dramatic change in nature on a cosmic scale. If something as large as the moon shows change, perhaps the entire universe is not as static as was once thought. Perhaps it did not always exist as it does today. Perhaps there was a creation after all.

Thus, Rosh Chodesh, the day when the moon begins its cycle anew, testifies that likewise the universe had a point of origin. It demonstrates that Hashem is the Creator of the universe. That is why one who blesses the new moon, who recognizes it as Hashem's signature on creation, is regarded as having greeted the Shechinah.[1]

Of Ibex and Hyrax

On Rosh Chodesh we recite the psalm "Barchi Nafshi."[2] One reason is that it includes the verse "He made the moon for the festivals...," an allusion to Rosh Chodesh.[3] An additional reason is tied to the theme of Rosh Chodesh being Hashem's mastery of creation. "Barchi Nafshi" describes the wonders of the universe, specifically from the perspective of having been created by Hashem.

A fascinating example of this is contained in the following verse from Barchi Nafshi:

> The high hills [are] for the ibex, the rocks as a refuge for the hyraxes.[4]
>
> (Tehillim 104:18)

Ibex are a species of wild goat with magnificent, curved horns that were used to make shofros for emergency fast days.[5] These spectacularly agile creatures are found in the rough hills of the Negev in Israel, especially in regions such as Ein Gedi and Avdat. Hyraxes live in rocky areas.

When enemies approach, they quickly dart down to hide among the rocks.

Typically, we would consider these animals ideally suited to their environment. Ibex, powerfully built but with short legs, are adept at negotiating steep hillsides, an ideal way of escaping predators. Hyraxes have sweat glands in their feet which assist in gripping the surface of rock, and long, tactile hairs at intervals over their bodies which help them feel their way inside dark fissures and tunnels. Both species show perfect adaptation to their terrain.

This perspective, however, is entirely false, based on a century of Darwinian propaganda. We know that

"If the high hills were created for the ibex, how much more so was the entire world created in the merit of Avraham Avinu!" (Midrash Tehillim 104).

Hashem created the world and that there is a hierarchy in creation. Man, as the goal of creation, is the most important creature. Following man come animals, and then come plants and inanimate matter. Ibex are therefore more important than terrain. Hashem created the terrain to suit the ibex. The high hills are *for* the ibex, created specifically to suit their needs.[6] The rocks are *for* the hyraxes. The habitat is purposefully adapted to the animals, not the other way around.[7]

The Women's Festival

> On Rosh Chodesh, one is permitted to perform *melachah* [creative actions]; those women who customarily do not perform *melachah* have a commendable practice.
>
> (*Shulchan Aruch, Hilchos Rosh Chodesh* 1)

Rosh Chodesh is the "women's holiday." One reason for this dates back to the sin of the golden calf. When the men willingly engaged in constructing and worshiping the calf, the women refused to donate their jewelry for the task. In reward for their dedication to Hashem, Rosh Chodesh became a quasi-festival for women.[8]

The lunar month has clear significance for women in the realm of the physical world. The *niddah* (menstrual) cycle does not just happen to be a similar length of time to the lunar cycle. It is fundamentally linked to the lunar cycle; in many cases it is the exact same length. A 1959 study, relying on an enormous database, found the average length of the *niddah* cycle to be 29½ days, precisely the length of the lunar month.[9] The same study found the average length of gestation to be 265.8 days, exactly nine lunar months. Indeed, the Haggadah refers to the gestation period as "the nine lunar months of gestation." (The researchers themselves were puzzled, for there was no apparent reason for such a correlation; this caused other scientists to dismiss the identical time lengths as coincidence.)

The moon itself is considered conceptually to be the wife of the sun. It unites with the sun by taking in its light and reflecting it toward us. In this way, it illustrates the relationship of Hashem to the Jewish people, which is also presented as a husband-wife relationship. We find that Hashem's life-giving radiance is meta-

The word shemesh, "sun," is in the masculine gender, and levanah, "moon," is feminine.

phorically described in terms of the sun:

For the sun and shield is Hashem...

(Tehillim 84:12)

We receive our life force from Hashem and reflect it to the rest of the world. Thus, the joy and dancing associated with the sanctification of the new moon, when the moon begins again to take in the sunlight, is that of a wedding celebration.[10]

King David

דוד מלך ישראל חי וקים.

David, king of Israel, lives and endures!

(Kiddush Levanah)

Rabbi Yehudah HaNasi used this phrase from Kiddush Levanah as a code to mark the declaration of Rosh Chodesh (Rosh HaShanah 25a).

Davidic kingship is a central theme of Rosh Chodesh.[11] (Note, too, that the above quote in Hebrew and the words *rosh chodesh* have identical numerical values.[12]) The kingship of David and his descendants is comparable to the waxing and waning of the moon in that it undergoes periods of triumph and periods of decline. The analogy is precise: The moon increases in size for fifteen days, then decreases for the same period. There were fifteen generations from Avraham to Shlomo HaMelech in which the nation rose to a peak of greatness. For the fifteen generations from Shlomo HaMelech to Tzidkeyah, the nation underwent a decline, resulting in the destruction of the first Beis HaMikdash in Tzidkeyah's time.[13]

"[David's] seed shall endure forever... It shall be established forever like the moon..." (Tehillim 89:37–38).

More fundamentally, the moon itself, by reflecting the sun's light to Earth, represents the concept of kingship. The role of a Jewish king is not absolute sovereignty. The king is designated as a representative of Hashem, the King of kings. The king is charged with reflecting Hashem's authority onto the people.[14]

Renewal and Redemption

The moon vanishes from sight. All is dark. But suddenly the moon appears anew, to cast its light on us again. So, too, the Jewish people are in the darkness of exile. But our relationship with Hashem will be renewed someday in its full glory, when He redeems us from exile and restores the Davidic kingship:

> *The voice of my Beloved! Behold, He comes...*
> (Shir HaShirim 2:12, recited in *Kiddush Levanah*)

"To the moon He said that it should renew itself as a crown of splendor..." (Kiddush Levanah). This refers to the crown of Davidic kingship (Eitz Yosef).

קציר

SPRING HARVEST

NISSAN

Starting Afresh

החדש הזה לכם ראש חדשים.

This month shall be for you as the head of the months.
(Shemos 12:2)

The cycle of months begins with Rosh Chodesh Nissan. Every Rosh Chodesh contains the power of renewal, as manifest in the renewal of the moon. Rosh Chodesh Nissan, the crown of all Roshei Chadashim, contains an extra-special power of renewal. This is manifest in the renewal of the entire natural world at this time. Refreshed by the rains of winter, the plants and animals all begin a new cycle of growth.

With the advent of Nissan, we enter the season of *katzir,* "spring harvest." During the coming few months, the different crops will be ripening, and the land will be a bustle of intense harvesting activity. First to ripen is the barley crop. The more important wheat crop will ripen two months later, during the Shavuos period, the Festival of Harvest.

"On Pesach, judgment is passed on the crops"
(Rosh HaShanah 16a).

Spring is a special time of rejuvenation at all levels. Nissan launches the ability for the Jewish people and the entire natural world in general to renew themselves. This power had the greatest effect during the Exodus, when we were transformed into a nation overnight.

The Sprouting of Redemption

For as the earth brings forth her growth [tzimchah], and as the garden causes that which was planted in it to sprout, so Hashem my God will cause righteousness and praise to sprout forth [yatzmiach] before all the nations.

(Yeshayahu 61:11)

Nissan is the month of redemption. This was signified by the Exodus from Mitzrayim, and it shall be highlighted most clearly with the coming of Mashiach, which will take place in Nissan.[1] The process of redemption is called *tzemichah*, "sprouting," which is what occurs in nature at this time. If we look at nature, we will be able to understand this parallel more clearly.

Were it not for our prior knowledge of botany, the springtime sprouting of plants would come as quite a shock. The last we saw of the seeds was their apparent decomposition into the ground, battered by the harsh winter weather. There appeared to be no hope for new life. Now we see that a new beginning was in the making. The very decomposition of the seed was actually the formation of new life. The shoot was slowly developing, and now it bursts forth from the ground.

"Blessed are You, Hashem, Who causes the pride of redemption to sprout" (Shemoneh Esreh).

Such is the case with the Jewish people.[2] The exile is long and bitter and seems as though it will never end. But the suffering itself, the spiritual purification of the Jewish people, is part of the redemption process. Beneath the surface, the seeds of salvation are germinating. One day Mashiach, also called *Tzemach*,[3] will sprout forth.

"Behold, days are coming," says Hashem, "...when I will cause an offshoot [tzemach] of righteousness to grow for David, and he shall ensure justice and righteousness in the land."

(Yirmeyahu 33:14–15)

Birth and Rebirth

The month of Nissan has a special name in the Torah — *chodesh heAviv. Aviv*, usually translated as "spring," is based on the word *av*, "father" or "originator."[4] At this time of year the land "gives birth" to new life in the form of emerging plants, crops, and flowers. This was made possible by the life-giving rains of winter. We have already learned about the concept of the rain being "male" and the land being "female." Together, they become the "parents" of all the ensuing growth.

"Today you are leaving, in the month of Aviv" (Shemos 13:4).

In a similar way, the Jewish people experience a process of (re)birth at this time. It was at this time of year, long ago in Mitzrayim, that the nation was born. This is the way Moshe describes the Exodus, when he challenges the children of Yisrael to find a similar event in history:

See if anything as great as this has ever happened... Has God ever performed miracles, to bring one nation from within another nation?

(Devarim 4:32, 34)

The Maharal[5] notes that the words "from within another nation" are meant as a metaphor for the process of the Exodus. This was similar to childbirth, where the child is taken from inside its mother. In Nissan we were born; in Nissan we are reborn, every year.

The greatest rebirth of all will be experienced with

the coming of Mashiach, in Nissan. This is not due merely to Nissan's historic significance for the Jewish people. It is due to the very nature of this month providing the *ability* for rebirth and renewal. In Nissan we were redeemed; in Nissan we shall be redeemed.

The rebirth of Mashiach will not occur only for nationhood. There will also be the resurrection of the dead. Just as the plants undergo a rebirth in spring, so will previous members of the Jewish people be born again.

Born Free

Pesach is *zeman cheiruseinu*, "the time of our freedom," the time in which we were redeemed from slavery in Mitzrayim. Everyone understands this to be a main theme of the Exodus. But what exactly *is* freedom? The answer to this question is not as simple as one might think.

Freedom is usually taken to mean the availability of options. People strive for the freedom of choice, the ability to choose from as many options as possible. But we are concerned here with an entirely different meaning of freedom.

Freedom can also refer to the ability to pursue the course one wishes to follow, without hindrance from any obstructions or restrictions.[6] We speak of a machine part moving freely or of someone being freed from prison. In this context, the focus is not on the availability of choice — it is on the ability to proceed with whatever choice has been made.

In the same way, the freedom we celebrate on Pesach is the freedom to pursue our path of Divine service. In Mitzrayim we had the Divine spark literally crushed out of us. The word *mitzrayim* is based on the root *meitzar*, "limitation" or "confinement." The evil forces of Mitzrayim prevented us from spiritual growth. The Exodus from Mitzrayim resulted in freedom from any restrictions on our course of spiritual growth. We were able to proceed with mitzvos — the sanctification of the months, the *korban Pesach*, and ultimately the receiving of the Torah at Sinai.

The spiritual forces of freedom present at this time of year are manifest in spring:

> *The voice of my Beloved! Behold, He comes leaping upon the mountains, skipping upon the hills. My Beloved is like a gazelle or a young hart; behold, He stands behind our wall, He looks in at the windows, He peers in through the lattice.*
>
> *My Beloved spoke and said to me, "Rise up, My beloved, My beautiful one, and go forth. For behold, the winter is over; the rains are past and gone. The shoots appear on the ground, the time of song has arrived, and the voice of the turtledove is heard in our land. The fig tree puts out her green figs, and the vines in blossom give their scent. Arise, My beloved, My beautiful one, and go forth!"*

(Shir HaShirim 2:8–13)

In spring nature frees itself from the shackles and suppression of winter. Now that the pounding rains and freezing cold are gone, nature can emerge in all its glory. The plants burst forth out of the ground. The word used here for "shoots," *nitzanim*, refers to something that breaks through.[7] Some relate the word *nissan* to *nitzan* with the same idea: emerging, springing free.[8] Spring is when the animals emerge from hibernation and the birds return from their migration. Spring is when the natural world springs free, unhindered by any restrictions to growth.

Rashi explains that the word used to describe the vines, semodar, refers to the grapes freeing themselves and emerging from the surrounding flower.

Barley: Poor but Carefree

On Pesach, the *omer* offering is brought from the newly ripened barley crop. Barley is used primarily for animal fodder. Wheat, on the other hand, will not ripen until Shavuos. It will then be brought as the offering of "two loaves." Wheat is the most important grain and is used to make bread for human consumption. The transition of *sefiras ha'omer* from Pesach to Shavuos is therefore represented by the transition from barley, a crop of low status, to wheat, a crop of high status. It demonstrates the growth and improvement man must undergo during this period.

Barley also relates to the type of freedom we've been discussing. It is of a very simple structure. Unlike wheat, whose kernel is surrounded by several layers of husk and chaff, barley has only one layer of husk. It is free of any other attachments.

Barley therefore also symbolizes poverty.[9] Free-

dom is often related to poverty — not in the negative sense, but in the sense of having no attachments to anything else. The poor man is free from possessions and duties. We may think wealth grants freedom, but it usually carries with it the burden of financial management. A car enables one to travel, but it comes with the hassle of insurance and maintenance, preventing one from living a truly carefree life. It is in this aspect of poverty that matzah is called *lechem oni*, "bread of poverty." Matzah is a very simple food, free from extraneous ingredients.[10] Conceptually similar to the freedom of barley, matzah is integral to the freedom of spring. Some relate the word *matzah* to the root *nitzah*, "springing free."[11]

The sheaf of barley says (Tehillim 102:1), "A prayer for the pauper, when he clothes himself and pours out his speech before Hashem" (Perek Shirah).

Barley is the fastest crop to ripen. It thereby also demonstrates *zerizus,* "zeal," a major motif of Nissan.

Shooting Forwards

For seven days you shall eat matzos, the bread of poverty, because you went out of Mitzrayim with haste...

(Devarim 16:3)

...And you shall eat [the korban Pesach] with haste; it is Pesach to Hashem.

(Shemos 12:12)

The Torah considers haste a central component of Pesach. We left Mitzrayim in a tremendous hurry — the Egyptians were desperate for us to get out as fast as possible. We baked our bread with haste. We have to eat the *korban Pesach* quickly. Let us explore why this speed was so essential to the process of the Exodus.

The Exodus from Mitzrayim, amidst Hashem's open miracles, represented the formation of the Jewish people and was one of the holiest moments in history. When we state that it was holy, we mean that it was uniquely connected to the higher spiritual worlds.

Space and time are dimensions unique to our physical world. They do not exist in the higher spiritual worlds. Where these worlds meet, the distinctions between them blur somewhat. At the interface, the point of close contact between our world and the spiritual worlds, the dimensions of space and time begin to warp.[12]

An example will make this clear. Let us consider the dimension of space. Eretz Yisrael is the holiest country in the world. Within Eretz Yisrael, Yerushalayim is the holiest city. Within Yerushalayim, the holiest place is the site of the Beis HaMikdash. And within the Beis HaMikdash, the holiest point in space, the interface to spirituality, is the site of the *Aron HaKodesh*, the Holy Ark.

Now, working inward, we find that space is progressively distorted as one moves toward the *Aron*. The gazelle is used as a metaphor for Eretz Yisrael, for just as a gazelle's skin seems too small to have covered its body, so does Eretz Yisrael seem too small to contain its inhabitants.[13] Moving further inward, we find a greater degree of distortion: despite Yerushalayim being packed with pilgrims for the three festivals, we are told that no one ever complained that it was too crowded.[14] On the grounds of the Beis HaMikdash, space is warped even more: the massed crowds on Yom Kippur were tightly packed together, yet when they prostrated themselves, they all had plenty of room to do so.[15] The site of the *Aron* itself was completely removed from the dimension of space — it took up no space at all. The

Aron was two and a half cubits wide; although the Sanctuary, in which it was situated, was twenty cubits wide, there were still ten cubits from each side of the *Aron* to the Sanctuary walls.[16]

The same is true of time. The Exodus, one of the holiest moments in history, was uniquely connected to the higher spiritual worlds, where there is no time. As the interface, the Exodus occurred in a "time warp," taking place in an unnaturally brief length of time.[17] Two hundred and ten years of slavery ended literally overnight, with millions of people marching out of bitter exile. This event was unique in the history of the world — according to the normal rules, such a thing simply cannot happen.

The name Nissan is related to the word nes, "miracle"; it signifies the transcendental nature of this month.

This is how spirituality is attained — with haste to minimize unnecessary time, with zeal and alacrity, striving to connect with the higher worlds. This, too, is the message of matzah:

> *And you shall guard the matzos...*
>
> (Shemos 12:17)

> Rabbi Yeshayah said: "Don't read, *You shall guard the matzos*; read instead, *You shall guard the mitzvos.* Just as one does not allow matzos to become leavened, so too one should not allow mitzvos to become 'leavened.' If an opportunity arises to perform a mitzvah, perform the mitzvah immediately."
>
> (*Mechilta, Maseches D'Pischa* 9)

If an action is to be spiritual, as a mitzvah should be, it must be performed with zeal and not allowed to grow stale. That is the message of matzah — we must act with alacrity and waste no time. Matzah, with the addition of just a few extra moments, becomes *chametz.* A few moments make all the difference.

Spring is when nature speeds up. The shoots appear on the ground, growing at an unparalleled rate. The animals scurry around in a flurry of activity, making the most of their newly found freedom. Young creatures develop with great speed. The natural world hastily tries to maximize its benefit from the combination of the winter waters with the spring warmth; it has only recently become warm enough to grow, and the life-giving waters of winter will soon dry up beneath the blazing summer sun. The spirituality of this season warps time for nature. If we are sensitive to the frenzied activity going on around us at this time, we can benefit from this energy ourselves.

The zeal in nature is expressed in terms of rapid *growth*. We, too, are enjoined to use the power of speed in this area, as we shall discover from the nature of Pesach.

Springing Up

Pesach is a time when we are able to zoom up through levels of growth normally acquired slowly. The greatest use of this ability came at the time of the Exodus. We had sunk to the forty-ninth level of impurity, nearly to the point of no return. And in no time at all we shot up to become the nation of Hashem. The spectacular miracles Hashem used to bring us out of Mitzrayim boosted us to extraordinary spiritual heights. Ordinarily, one must painstakingly move through the levels of growth, slowly and surely. But Pesach is something different. It had to be.

The voice of my Beloved! Behold, He comes leaping upon the mountains, skipping upon the hills. My Beloved is like a gazelle or a young hart...

(Shir HaShirim 2:8–10)

The people said to Moshe: "How can we be redeemed? Surely Hashem swore to Avraham that we would be enslaved for four hundred years..." He replied: "Since Hashem wants to redeem you, He will ignore the details..." They said: "But we lack good deeds." He replied: "Since Hashem wants to redeem you, He will not look at your bad deeds..."

(*Shir HaShirim Rabbah* loc. cit.)

Hashem skipped the technical details and redeemed us before it was too late. The national birth of the Exodus was an induced birth!

As an unborn creature in its mother's womb which the shepherd pulls out, so did God take one nation from inside another nation.

(Based on *Midrash Shocher Tov*, Tehillim 116)

He passed over the calculations of the exile, He passed over the fact that we were unworthy. He skipped straight to the moment of the Exodus. In turn, we were granted the power to skip ahead. For we were not yet deserving of the miraculous nature of the Exodus. We were treated by Hashem as though we were on an extremely high level, leaping to spiritual levels at a rate that has not been equaled before or since. The very name of this festival, *Pesach*, which means "pass over," alludes to this special ability to leap through levels of growth at this time of year.

Nature uses this ability to its fullest. The power of leaping is not just manifest in gazelles skipping over hills. It is expressed in the entire natural world progressing at its greatest growth rate, springing ahead in the glory of spring. The crops are rapidly developing and ripening. The birds' eggs hatch into chicks which in a matter of weeks are fully feathered and able to fly. Frog spawn becomes aquatic, fish-like tadpoles, which grow legs and lose their gills to become terrestrial animals. We may take this for granted, but it is nothing short of a miraculous transformation if we stop and ponder it. And it is a development that takes place with almost unbelievable speed.

If we sensitize ourselves to this energy, we too can spring through levels of growth. We can emulate our ancestors' development, when they leaped from being a crushed, slave people to being crowned Hashem's nation, expressing His glory.

Freedom of Expression

"The tongue is the quill of the heart and the emissary of the mind" (Chovos HaLevavos, Sha'ar HaBechinah 5).

The exile in Mitzrayim is sometimes referred to as *galus hadibbur,* "exile of speech," with the Exodus being the "exodus of speech." *Dibbur,* "speech," is the tool man uses to express himself. Feelings, thoughts, ideas, everything of value to man, finds its mode of expression through speech. Man is supposed to use this power of expression to express the glory of Hashem.

The opposite of *ex*pression is *sup*pression. This was Mitzrayim, whose name, as we explained, is based on the word *meitzar,* "limited" or "suppressed." Mitzrayim suppressed our Jewishness. Pharaoh used every means possible to break us — giving us hard labor, splitting up families, preventing us from keeping mitzvos. This, the obstruction of religious expression, is called the "exile of speech." Therefore, the Exodus from Mitzrayim was the freedom of speech. We were now able to perform mitzvos, such as the sanctification of the month and the *korban Pesach.* We were free to voice our status as the select nation of Hashem.[18]

The aforementioned paragraph in Shir HaShirim describes this theme beautifully:

The time of song has arrived, and the voice of the turtledove is heard in our land...

(Shir HaShirim 2:12)

In spring, nature expresses itself in all its glory. The frogs, arriving back at their pond to breed, are croaking. The crickets are rubbing their legs and wings together to produce their musical chirping. Most noticeable of all, the birds sing in an orchestra of different voices. The distinct *turrr* sound of the turtledove (called *tur* in the Torah) can be heard as they return from their winter migration. Nature uses this month's special potential for speech to express its splendor, to sing aloud the glory of Hashem. Even the crops appear

to sing, as the ripe ears of grain rustle in the wind:[19]

The hills are clothed with sheep, the valleys are covered with grain, they shout for joy, they sing (Tehillim 65:14) ...When do the sheaves sing? In Nissan...

(*Rosh HaShanah* 8a)

In truth, all of nature sings at this time — even the silent participants. Their very splendor at this time of year is the finest expression of nature's inner beauty, singing the glory of the Creator. The delicate charm of a tiny flower, the ripples of a brook, and the skillful maneuvers of the ibex on the rocky hills are all expressions of Hashem's glory.

This is one of the energies of Pesach, whose name is a compacted form of the words *peh sach*, "the mouth speaks." This is the power we take advantage of every year with the mitzvah of reciting and discussing the Haggadah, which literally means "speaking." Pesach is the time to express the potential of the Divine spark that burns within us all. The sounds of spring demonstrate the unique potential for expression available at this time of year, a potential we must use to the best of our abilities. As we say in the Haggadah, "Anyone who increases his discussing of the Exodus is praiseworthy."[20]

Bird Song

It is specifically *song* which is highlighted by the paragraph in Shir HaShirim. *Shirah* is a highly significant version of speech and therefore a central aspect of Nissan. Song is a uniquely powerful mode of expression, providing room for an entirely new dimension of depth and emotion. We used this power when

we crossed the Reed Sea, an event we relive every year on the seventh day of Pesach when we read the *shirah* in that day's Torah reading.

The significance of *shirah* on Pesach can also be seen in the reading of megillas Shir HaShirim. The verses in Shir HaShirim draw our attention to the songs of the birds, which is especially prevalent in spring. There are conceptual relationships between song and birds beyond that of their being the most musical creatures. We find that *shirah* is also referred to in conjunction with the word *kanaf*, "wing":[21]

מכנף הארץ זמרת שמענו צבי לצדיק.

From the edge [literally, "wing"] of the earth we have heard songs, glory to the righteous...

(Yeshayahu 24:16)

Wings enable birds to leave the ground and ascend to the skies. In the same way, song enables man to elevate the low physicality of his earthly surroundings to lofty spiritual heights.

In the natural world, everything performs a unique function from which we can glean a unique lesson. The mighty lion teaches us the characteristic of strength. The swift gazelle demonstrates to us the attribute of alacrity. The simple barley illustrates the quality of freedom. However, it would be a mistake to think that these are merely parables for the lessons. These spiritual qualities have an earthly manifestation in terms of the animals and plants. The lion is the embodiment of the quality of strength. The gazelle is alacrity incarnate, and barley is freedom.

"Rabbi Yehudah ben Teimah said: 'Be as brazen as a leopard, as light as an eagle, as swift as a gazelle, and as mighty as a lion to perform the will of your Father in Heaven' " (Avos 5:24).

Thus, the physical elements of the natural world all have lofty spiritual roots. These lowly creatures and plants have a link to a far higher reality. The song of nature is its transcendence above earthliness.

But this song is revealed only by man. For it is only through man's free will that he can choose to learn lessons from the world. The *shirah* of nature comes about through man revealing the Divine spark that lies within every part of creation, thus elevating the natural world.[22]

The Song of Spring

A closer inspection of nature's song reveals that it is not only the different elements in the ecosystem that produce this harmony, but also the different stages in the cycle of time. Periods of growth, flowering — death, too — are all essential parts of this system. This gives us an additional insight into the song of spring.

Taking a closer look at the song we sang by the Reed Sea, we find that the Torah introduces it with an interesting choice of words:

Then Moshe sang this song...

(Shemos 15:1)

The Midrash explains that the word *then* refers to an incident that occurred while the Jewish people were slaves.[23] Following Hashem's orders, Moshe tried to persuade Pharaoh to release them, to no avail. Even worse, Pharaoh added to their workload and increased their hardships. Moshe returned to Hashem and pointed out that His instructions had not helped:

And from then, *my coming to Pharaoh to speak in Your name, he has worsened his evil toward this people, and You have not saved Your people.*

(Ibid. 5:22)

The Midrash states that this statement was an error on Moshe's part; he showed a lack of trust in Hashem. Moshe was questioning Hashem's handling of this unpleasant situation. It was only later, at the splitting of the Reed Sea, the culmination of the Exodus, that Moshe perceived how perfectly Hashem had planned matters. It was not only that Moshe appreciated the miracles that were currently saving the Jewish people. The point was that Moshe now recognized that even the exile had been for the best. He looked back at the hardships that caused him to doubt Hashem and saw that they had aided in the development of the nation and had set the stage for the majesty of the Exodus.

This is one of the key elements of *geulah* — recognizing that even the bad times were vital for achieving the good times. That is why at the seder we eat *maror* in a sandwich, between two pieces of matzah. *Maror*, the bitter herb, represents exile, while matzah represents freedom, as we have already learned. Consuming them together signifies our recognition that even the hardships of exile were an essential ingredient of the redemption.[24]

"A song of ascents; when Hashem returns the captives of Zion, we will have been as dreamers. Then our mouths will be full of laughter and our tongues with glad song" (Tehillim 126:1–2).

Therefore, it was the same term, *then*, that Moshe had used in his doubts, which he now used in the song by the sea. The word *then* is peculiar. It can refer to an event that has already happened, or to one that has not yet happened. In truth, the word *then* is outside time, linking past and future together. When one perceives the unity of history, seeing how every element falls into place, one expresses it with this word.[25] The song by the Sea of Reeds referred to the exile as much as it referred to the Exodus.[26]

This is the song of spring. The song is not sung merely by nature blossoming in all its glory. It is a song of the different stages of time showing their results. It was only a short while ago that we were trapped in the grip of winter. The heavy rains were a source of distress, and the stormy weather perhaps clouded our appreciation of how Hashem guides nature. Yet now, as the earth explodes with life, we look back at winter and see it in a different light. If not for the abundance of rain, the plants would not be able to grow. If not for the dark season we went through, we would not be able to appreciate the brightness of spring. The song of spring is sung about the winter, too. For the beauty of spring is the harmony of summer, autumn, and winter.

Spring of the Gazelle

Many of the themes we have identified in Nissan are expressed in the creature highlighted by our paragraph in Shir HaShirim:

> *The voice of my Beloved! Behold, He comes leaping upon the mountains, skipping upon the hills. My Beloved is like a gazelle or a young hart; behold, He stands behind our wall, He looks in at the windows, He peers in through the lattice.*
>
> (Shir HaShirim 2:12)

" 'And I shall give you a desirable land, a heritage of tzvi...' (Yirmeyahu 3:19). Just as a gazelle is swift in its pace, so is Eretz Yisrael swift to produce fruit..." (Kesubos 112a).

The beautiful gazelle, called *tzvi* in the Torah,[27] encapsulates the season of spring. Though gazelles are still very common in the hills around Jerusalem, most people have never seen them. For those who have seen them, it is usually just a glimpse of a rapidly disappearing tail. Their extreme swiftness is the reason, a fleetness of foot which is a perfect example of *zerizus*, "alacrity." It is this aspect of the gazelle's nature that we are enjoined to emulate:

> Be as swift as a gazelle...to fulfill the desire of your Father in Heaven.
>
> *(Avos 5:24)*

In a more mystical sense, the gazelle represents the concept of freedom from physical constraints and restrictions.[28] The gazelle is barely contained within the physical plane. Its extreme delicacy of form makes it seem more spiritual than physical. In its leaping gait, it seems to be trying to break the bonds of gravity. One form of the gazelle's motion, unique to this creature, involves the gazelle springing from the ground with all four legs simultaneously. It seems to be breaking free from earthliness, from physicality.

"The gazelle always sleeps with one eye open" (Yalkut Shimoni 720). The watchful nature of this animal is a prerequisite to zerizus: "Watchfulness leads to zeal" (Avodah Zarah 20b).

The Maharal[29] notes that this concept is apparent in the gazelle's name. *Tzvi* is a synonym for *pe'er*, "spiritual splendor" or "transcendence." The lithe and delicate gazelle seems to transcend the physical constraints of this world.

The gazelle expresses the *zerizus*, freedom, and transcendence of the redemption for which we yearn:

> *Flee, my beloved, and be like a gazelle...*
>
> (Shir HaShirim 8:14)

Just as the gazelle journeys to the end of the world but returns to its place, so too Yisrael, though they are scattered throughout the world, are destined to return, as it is written, *I shall go; I shall return to my place* (Hoshea 5:15).

(Yalkut Shimoni loc. cit.)

Dew of Kindness

I shall be as dew to Yisrael; he shall blossom like a lily...
(Hoshea 14:6)

On Pesach, we recite the prayer for dew. The rainy season may be over, but water is still provided in the form of dew. The dew that falls on the plants during the night is of great value. Despite the doubts formerly expressed by some scientists as to its benefits, recent research has confirmed its importance. In fact, the fertility of many parts of Eretz Yisrael is due to the abundance of dew in those areas.[30]

Dew is not merely a lighter form of rain. It is of a very different nature. A proper understanding of the difference between the two is essential for understanding the differences between the summer months (Nissan to Elul) and the winter months (Tishrei to Adar).

Rain is extremely aperiodic. A year's rainfall can be good, resulting in excellent crops, or poor, resulting in economic disaster and possibly famine. Hashem allots the amount of rainfall in direct accordance with our actions, giving us a heavy rainfall only if we deserve it. At times of severe national punishment, the rains may be withheld altogether. The winter rains are an example of the attribute of *din*, "strict judgment," which predominates at that time of year.

Dew, on other hand, represents the summer months' quality of *chesed*:

...as dew from Hashem, as the drops on the grass, which are not hoped for by man nor awaited by people.

(Michah 5:6)

How do we know dew is not withheld? When Eliyahu swore to Achav that there would be a drought, the dew still fell (Ta'anis 3a).

Dew is never withheld.[31] It always falls in approximately the same amounts. As such, it is a demonstration of Hashem's *chesed*, "kindness." Even if we sin, Hashem grants us dew. Here we see again a theme mentioned earlier — that Nissan is a time when Hashem grants us gifts that we do not necessarily deserve. At the time of the Exodus, we were assisted by miracles that we did not yet deserve. Every year at this time, we are granted special spiritual energies regardless of whether or not we are worthy of them. The dew is another example of a Divine gift that does not come as a result of our actions.[32]

At the final redemption, the ultimate kindness of the resurrection of the dead[33] will take place through dew:

> How do we know that there is no *techiyas hameisim* except through dew? It is written, *The dead ones of your people shall live; my dead body shall arise. Wake up and sing, you who dwell in dust, for your dew is the dew of Light...* (Yeshayahu 26:19).
>
> (*Yerushalmi, Ta'anis 2a*)

Arrival of the Stork

The stork usually passes through Eretz Yisrael during the week of parashas Shemini in spring and during the week of parashas Re'eh in the fall; these are the two parashiyos in which it is mentioned (Zimras HaAretz V'HaShamayim on Perek Shirah).

The stork in the skies also knows her appointed time; and the turtledove, the swift, and the crane observe the time of their coming...

(Yirmeyahu 8:7)

In Nissan, the skies of Eretz Yisrael are full of birds.[34] Because this tiny strip of land is on the main migration route to and from Africa, it is home to a disproportionately large number of birds each spring. They each know "their appointed time...the time of their coming."

The stork[35] in particular is highlighted. It is particularly conspicuous in Nissan, as vast flocks of these large, graceful birds circle the sky, rising steadily on hot air thermals. But the stork is significant here for another reason. It is called *chasidah* in the Torah, based on the word *chesed*. It is so called partly because it treats its fellow storks with affection.[36] As such, it relates to the *chesed* which is so much a theme of this month.[37]

Most important of all, the arrival of the stork is the welcome herald of spring after a harsh winter. It demonstrates that even the dark periods of life will be followed by the *chesed* of salvation:

> The stork says, *Speak to the heart of Jerusalem and call to her, for her time has arrived, for her sins have been pardoned, for she has taken double [punishment] from Hashem's hand for all her sins* (Yeshayahu 40:2).
>
> (*Perek Shirah*)

Spring Morning

להגיד בבוקר חסדך...

To relate of Your kindness in the morning...

(Tehillim 92:3)

With the day being a microcosm of the year, the verse is not only noting the *chesed* that predominates in the morning; it is also noting the order of *chesed* present in spring, the "morning" section of the year. The renewal of the morning, when Hashem, in His kindness, releases us from the darkness of night, is paralleled by the renewal of spring, when we emerge from the gloom of winter. The same *chesed* is found when Hashem will take us out from the long, dark night of exile to the bright morning of redemption.

And I will sing of Your kindness in the morning...

(Ibid. 59:17)

IYAR

Radiant Health

For those who fear My Name, there shall shine the healing sun of righteousness.

(Malachi 3:21)

The second month of the year, Iyar, is given a name in the Torah, *Ziv*,[1] which means "radiance." The name refers to the glorious state of the trees at this time.[2] The spectacular blossoms of Nissan bask in the warm summer sun, still fueled by the waters of winter.

Please, Hashem, heal her now, by showing her the pleasantness of Your *ziv*...

(*Yedid Nefesh*)

Iyar is a month uniquely suited to health and healing. The weather is ideal — warm enough to grant vitality, yet without the oppressive summer heat. The word *iyar* itself is an acronym of "I am Hashem, your Healer" (אני יקוק רפאיך).[3]

This power began when the Jewish people journeyed through the desert, miraculously sustained by

The manna was a physical incarnation of Hashem's ziv (Or Gedalyahu, Beshalach).

the manna. The manna, which began to fall during this month, was perfectly nutritious. It was so wholly beneficial that no waste products had to be expelled from the body after its consumption. This wonderful food cured all ailments and empowered this month forever with special healing powers.[4]

Every month is part of a pattern, connected to the months that precede it and follow it, and part of the growth cycle of the whole year. Iyar in particular is best viewed as a follow-up to Nissan and Pesach, and as a preparation for Sivan and Shavuos.[5] Iyar contains most of *sefiras ha'omer*, the count-up from Pesach to Shavuos.

As we investigate the nature of this month and the next one, we will focus primarily on the development of the wheat crop, which is steadily ripening at this time. Wheat is important, as it is used to make bread, the staple of man's diet. But let us now explore another facet of the significance of wheat.

The Wheat Crop

Your essence is [like] a heap of wheat.

(Shir HaShirim 7:4)

This refers to Yisrael.

(*Shir HaShirim Rabbah* 7:3)

There is a powerful lesson to be learned from wheat, taught by Rabbi Akiva to the wicked Roman leader, Turnus Rufus.[6] Turnus Rufus challenged Rabbi Akiva with a question: Which is greater, the work of Hashem or the work of man? He expected Rabbi Akiva to answer that the work of Hashem is greater. This answer would provide him with a basis for attacking the law of circumcision; for if Hashem chose to create man in a certain way, how can man dare try to improve on Hashem's work? Much to his surprise, however, Rabbi Akiva replied that the work of man is greater. He brought out some sheaves of wheat, the work of Hashem, and some fine pastries, the work of man. "Which are superior," he asked Turnus Rufus, "the sheaves or the pastries?"

Rabbi Akiva had proven that the work of man is superior. Defeated, Turnus Rufus asked another question: If a circumcised man is a more perfect being than an uncircumcised man, why did Hashem not create man in a circumcised state? Surely it was within His power to do so.

Rabbi Akiva's answer provides us a timeless lesson: Hashem deliberately created this world in an incomplete state, so man could perfect himself and the world. Man is enjoined to improve himself through

learning Torah and performing mitzvos. On a physical level, this task of self-perfection is performed through circumcision. On a higher level, man is supposed to constantly refine his mind and heart.

"And you shall remove [literally, 'circumcise'] the imperfections [literally, 'foreskin'] of your heart..." (Devarim 10:16).

Wheat projects this lesson most succinctly. The ground does not produce ready-baked bread; it produces the raw materials with which we are to work. Wheat will not be ready to eat upon harvesting. In fact, it requires more effort than any other crop before it is fit for the table. Many hours of different tasks — winnowing, kneading, baking — are required before it reaches its finished state. Its special potential is only realized after a great amount of effort.

We can see this parallel carried even further: each kernel of wheat is split, alluding to circumcision, the act of perfection man performs on himself.[7] Even more significant is that the blessing we pronounce on wheat changes as we refine it. On wheat in its raw state, one says the blessing *borei pri ha'adamah,* "Who creates the fruit of the earth." After we transform it into bread, its blessing changes to *hamotzi lechem min ha'aretz,* "Who produces bread from the ground," which exempts a person from saying a blessing on any other food he eats at his meal. This is a sign that the bread is of elevated status — through our effort with the wheat, it attains spiritual elevation. In the same way we can work on ourselves and attain spiritual elevation.

The Maturing Process

It was only a short while ago that the plant kingdom, enjoying the energy of the spring sun and the saturation of the winter rains, was leaping up through many

stages of growth. Now the rapid rate of growth that occurred during Nissan seems to have come to a halt. Closer
study, however, reveals that it is only the external growth
that has stopped. True, the wheat has reached its full size,
but it has not yet reached its full maturity. On the inside,
it is still growing, developing, ripening.

If we look to ourselves, we see the same pattern.
Pesach was a time of unnaturally rapid spiritual growth.
It was unnatural in a literal sense, as the normal rules of
human development simply do not allow for such rapid
strides, but on Pesach there was a special gift from
Above. The Jewish people at the time of the Exodus wit-
nessed Hashem performing incredible miracles, and
they were raised to a lofty spiritual level. Every year,
Pesach grants us the ability to leap up many rungs on
the ladder of spiritual growth. But it is not natural; it is a
gift from Hashem and does not come about through our
own efforts.

After the Exodus, the Jewish people traveled
through the barren desert toward Har Sinai. There were
no magnificent victories there, no seas to be split. It was
no longer easy to feel so intensely close to Hashem. In
our times, too, the special gift of inspiration we received
at Pesach leaves us, and the heights we scaled become
remote once again. In fact, whatever we do in life, things
often do not seem to go as well as they did when we
started. Why does this happen? Why doesn't Hashem
let us stay at our original state of inspiration?

The answer is that the only growth that really
counts is that which is achieved through our own efforts. It is not what one *is* that counts but what one
does. The rung on which a person was placed on the ladder of life is irrelevant; so, too, is the rung one is pushed

up to. It is how many rungs one climbs on the ladder that's important. Our purpose in life is to relate to Hashem. A genuine relationship has to be earned; it can never be presented as a gift.

Why, then, does Hashem give us this gift in the first place? The answer is clear: it is so much easier to work toward a goal when one has already tasted that goal. Once we have been made aware of the heights we can reach, we are better motivated and greater equipped to reach them again. But the work now must come from us; the level we attain is now dependent on our own efforts. We have to try to live up to that which we gained on Pesach. This is the process of *sefiras ha'omer*: developing, growing, working on a different aspect each day, to regain that original state.

The word chittah, "wheat," is related to the word chanatah, "first sprouting." Wheat reaches its first stages by itself; man must work on it to further transform it into bread (Shem MiShmuel, Ki Savo 5671).

Looking at the wheat crop, we see that our development is mapped out for us. The wheat stalks reached their full height during Nissan, but they did not yet "live up to it" — they had not yet matured. Now is the time when the wheat undergoes an internal maturing process, the stages of ripening.

The same pattern is reflected in the *mazalos* (the zodiac). The constellation of Nissan is the lamb, an animal which is led along by its owner. In Nissan we are led up the spiritual ladder by Hashem. The constellation of Iyar is the ox, an animal which uses its own strength to pull a load. Iyar is the month in which we use our own strength and efforts to earn this level. The key is to look back at the heights one scaled at the beginning and try to regain them. It will not be easy — it is not *supposed* to be easy — but that's where the real reward lies.

Grasping the Radiance

This concept gives us a fundamental understanding into why Iyar is called *Ziv*. *Ziv* usually refers to light in a specific form, when it radiates outward to an area beyond the source of light itself. Thus the rays of light that radiated from Moshe's face are called *ziv* by *Targum Onkelos*.[8]

The source of Light, of Revelation, is in Pesach, in Nissan. But that light is too bright, the month too miraculous. The levels we experience in Nissan are beyond us, far removed from what we are actually suited to perceive. The energies of Nissan are beyond our grasp.

Iyar is the means of grasping Nissan. The light of Nissan penetrates into Iyar, the month of Ziv.[9] The memories of Pesach serve to inspire us, to show us what we are working to achieve.

The Importance of the Individual

One might expect *sefiras ha'omer* to be an exciting time, as everyone joins in the buildup to receiving the Torah. However, its tone nowadays is anything but joyous. Since twenty-four thousand students of Rabbi Akiva died of a plague during *sefiras ha'omer*, it is customary to abstain from festivities during this time. Weddings are not celebrated, and haircuts are forbidden, in commemoration of the terrible tragedy. How can this be reconciled with such a wonderful month? Not only that, but this is supposed to be a month with unique health-giving properties! Why did they die in Iyar, of all times? How can we understand the strange duality of this month?

The reason given for their deaths is that they did not accord each other appropriate honor.[10] This problem may appear a slight one, but it was based on a flaw in their role as Torah students. They were designating the Torah as a very private, specialized discipline, instead of honoring everyone's input. They had not sufficiently internalized the concept that everyone has a uniquely important role to play. Iyar's astrological sign, the ox, represents focusing on one's own efforts, on one's own strength. The ox has its own strength — and he is proud of it. The students of Rabbi Akiva, too, were concerned with their own expertise in their specialized areas of study, failing to integrate properly with each other.

Wheat, so central to this time of year, teaches us about appreciating the importance of everyone:

Your essence is [like] a heap of wheat.

(Shir HaShirim 7:4)

Said Rabbi Yitzchak: "Just as wheat, when taken to be sown, is taken by number, and when brought in from the barn, it is brought in by number, so, too, when the children of Yisrael went down to Mitzrayim, they went down by number, as it is written, *As seventy souls did your fathers go down to Mitzrayim* (Devarim 10:22), and when they came up, they came up by number, as it says, *As six hundred thousand men...* (Shemos 12:37)."

(*Shir HaShirim Rabbah* 7:3)

A farmer does not care about how many haystacks he has. But the piles of wheat grain are counted precisely, for each one is important. This is the essence of the Jewish people: each member is to be treasured.[11]

Elixir of Life and Death

Iyar is a double-edged sword. It offers unique possibilities for growth in Torah and personal development. An outgrowth of this involvement with Torah, the source of life, is health. The Maharal[12] explains that Torah is a force of order in the universe, being the master plan. Absorption in Torah is therefore a cure for illnesses, which are disorders of the body. Attaching oneself to a force of order helps the body return to order, to health.

But for those who misuse the lessons of Iyar, the opposite occurs. Not only will the special health-giving properties of this month be unavailable, but the other extreme will manifest. The students of Rabbi Akiva died from plague, which killed through *askarah,* a disease of the throat.[13] The throat, the seat of the voice, is the tool of Torah communication. Their flawed approach to Torah caused them to suffer the harsh side of Iyar.[14]

> Rabbi Bena'ah said: "For the one who learns Torah *liShmah* [for its own sake], it will be an elixir of life... For the one who learns Torah not *liShmah*, it will be an elixir of death, as the verse says, *My doctrine shall pelt as the rain* (Devarim 32:2), and *pelting* always refers to killing..."
>
> (*Ta'anis* 7a)

Rain is usually a blessing, but if heavy rains fall during Iyar, it will batter the ripening crops.[15] The Torah is compared to water, a parable we shall explore later on. In this analogy, Torah is usually an elixir of life, but for the one who abuses it, it will destroy him.

One may wonder, though, in which way the sin of Rabbi Akiva's students — failing to value each other properly — bears any relation to not learning *liShmah*.

"Rainfall after Nissan has passed denotes a curse, as it is written (Shmuel I 12:17), 'Is it not the wheat harvest today? I shall call to Hashem, and He will send thunder and rain, and you shall know and see that your evil is great...'" (Ta'anis 2b).

To understand this, we shall explore another dimension of Iyar and the *omer*.

Kindness

N issan began an order of *chesed* (lovingkindness) in the year. In that month, Hashem granted us the spiritual gift of inspiration and the physical gift of dew. These gifts, granted regardless of whether or not we deserved them, demonstrate that Hashem is acting with His attribute of *chesed*. The period of *sefiras ha'omer* is a time in which we emulate this behavior, using this quality of kindness to build up ourselves and the world:

Omer has the same numerical value (310) as yeish, "existence."

> *The world is built by kindness...*
>
> (Tehillim 89:3)

Chesed requires man to ignore his personal desires and to selflessly dedicate himself to others. He must focus on giving rather than taking. It is during the *omer* that man must work on perfecting this trait. The numerical value of *omer*, 310, is ten times the numerical value of Hashem's name, א-ל, the name which represents His attribute of lovingkindness.[16] The tenfold multiplication signifies perfection and completion. During the *omer*, we engage in perfecting the quality of kindness, reaching perfection at Shavuos.

The quality of giving, and not focusing on one's own needs, is what lies behind the crops' development. The land is giving of its resources to the crops similar to the way human parents sustain their offspring. (This concept will be explored further in "Sivan.")

Rabbi Elazar said: "What is the meaning of *...and a Torah of kindness is on her tongue* (Mishlei 31:26)? Is there a Torah of kindness and a Torah that is not of kindness? Rather, studying Torah *liShmah* is considered a Torah of kindness; learning it for ulterior motives is not a Torah of kindness." Some say that learning in order to teach others is a Torah of kindness...

(*Sukkah* 49b)

"A Torah of kindness" means a Torah built on the quality of giving. One manifestation of this quality lies in the willingness to teach others. Another manifestation is found in the study of Torah *liShmah*. Learning Torah for its own sake means that I am not thinking about my personal needs and desires. I am not learning Torah for prestige, or to gain a reputation for wisdom, or so that I can be the world's greatest authority in a particular field. I am learning Torah entirely *for its own sake*.

That is the nature of Torah *liShmah*. That is the type of Torah which is an elixir of life — Torah based on thinking not about oneself, but about others. The students of Rabbi Akiva were not adequately selfless. They were not sufficiently concerned for each other's honor. For the one who fails to learn Torah *liShmah*, for the one who is too concerned with his own needs and importance, it becomes an elixir of death.

Iyar has unique properties. We must focus on giving of ourselves to Hashem and to others. Then our Torah learning will truly be an elixir of health and life.

קיץ
HIGH SUMMER

SIVAN

The Precious Fig

The season of high summer is called "*kayitz*" in the Torah, referring to the harvesting of figs which begins at this time (*kayitz* is based on the word *kitzah*, "cut").[1] Figs are unusual in that they do not all ripen at the same time. Some ripen in Sivan, while others ripen later, over the course of the summer. The harvest begins in Iyar, so the first ripe figs don't spoil, and extends over the next three or four months. Because they are the first fruit to ripen, figs are the first of the seven species to be brought as *bikkurim*, the first ripe fruits of the season.

Sivan is the month in which the Jewish people received the Torah. It is appropriate, therefore, that figs are used as a metaphor for Torah:

The one who guards the fig tree shall eat of her fruits.

(Mishlei 27:18)

Why are the words of the Torah compared to a fig tree? For just as whenever one searches a fig tree, one finds [ripe] figs, so too, whenever one learns Torah one finds new insights.

(*Eiruvin* 54a)

...Just as the fig tree is harvested gradually, so too is the Torah studied gradually, for it cannot all be learned in one or two years.

(Bemidbar Rabbah 21:15)

"If one sees a fig in a dream, his Torah is guarded within him" *(Berachos 57a).*

The verse in Mishlei speaks of the need to *guard* the fig tree. More than any other fruit tree, the fig requires guarding. It is usually planted at the edges of gardens and orchards, easily accessible to passersby. In addition, because the figs ripen over an extended period, they are vulnerable longer than other fruits. Finally, once a fig ripens, it spoils quickly. Unless the owner rises at dawn to harvest the figs that ripened during the night, the figs will rot or be damaged by birds and wasps. Only the one who expends effort in guarding his figs will eat the fruit.

In this respect the fig alludes to the Torah. The process of learning Torah is entirely different from any other academic process, like learning mathematics or chemistry. Not only must Torah be constantly reviewed, but it also requires purity of mind, as well as a host of other qualities.[2] Studying Torah requires one to be constantly alert and guard oneself.

The Midrash also uses the verse in Mishlei to explain why Yehoshua was selected to succeed Moshe rather than Moshe's sons:

> Moshe said,... "Surely my sons should inherit my position?" Hashem said to him: *"The one who guards the fig tree shall eat of her fruits...* Yehoshua looked after your needs, accorded you honor, and arose early and stayed late in your house of meeting; he arranged the benches and spread the cloths..."
>
> *(Bemidbar Rabbah* 21:14)

If a person is to be a true student, he must dedicate himself to his teacher absolutely, attentive to his every need. Then one is worthy to "eat of his fruit" — to absorb his teachings and transmit them to others.

Earthman

Man is called *"adam,"* because he was formed from *adamah*, "earth." This sounds straightforward enough, until we consider that cats and dogs and duckbilled platypuses were also formed from the earth! Every creature was formed from *adamah* — why does only man receive the name *adam*?

The Maharal[3] explains that there is a conceptual similarity between man and earth. Consider a patch of bare earth. It appears to be featureless, lifeless. One can dig, and one will still find nothing more exciting than soil. But if one waits and watches, one will witness an incredible phenomenon. Plants and flowers will grow seemingly out of nothing. Even huge trees can develop — and where does their bulk come from? The earth has a tremendous hidden potential within it; there is so much more than meets the eye.

Let us now consider animals. An animal is referred to in the Torah as בהמה (*beheimah*). This word is comprised of the words בה מה (*bah mah*), which mean "what is it?" or "what's in it?" or, as we might say, "what you see is what you get." What you see in an animal — its skin, eyes, limbs, and fur — is all there is to it. There are no hidden depths to a hippopotamus.

But man has the ability to develop his intellect and to perform acts of a genuinely altruistic nature. He can engage in spiritual growth, transforming himself into an ever-superior being. There is so much more to man than meets the eye. That is why he is named after earth. Man and earth are similar in that both contain tremendous hidden potential.

When does earth fulfill its potential? In the early summer, many animals and plants, born in the spring, reach their full size. Most importantly, it is at this time that wheat, that most significant of crops, reaches its final maturity and is finally ready to be made into bread. At this time, too, man reaches a stage of completion. It is in Sivan, with the acceptance of the Torah on Shavuos, that man achieves maturity. Torah is the ultimate tool for developing the intellect and the greatest source of wisdom. The Torah trains a person to have the highest morals and to differentiate himself from the animals. It brings out the human potential from his animal body. Just as the wheat is finally ripe and able to be made into bread, so is man finally complete and able to develop in Torah and mitzvos.

The Final Stage

One might easily make the mistake of thinking that the stage of completion already occurred in Nissan. After all, nothing much *appears* to have changed in nature since then. However, the wheat only appeared to have reached its full development in Nissan — externally, it reached its full size, but it had not yet ripened internally. It is only now, in Sivan, that the internal maturity matches the external size. The second stage, ripening, finally catches up with the first stage of rapid exterior growth.

This is the final stage in the pattern of man's development that we began to trace in Nissan. Shavuos is viewed as the final part of a sequence that began with Pesach and proceeded with *sefiras ha'omer*. In fact, Shavuos is not given a date in the Torah; it is identified as coming fifty days after Pesach. It must be viewed as the conclusion to what we began on Pesach. At that time, we rose to dizzying spiritual heights, through a special inspiration from Hashem. We grew at a spectacular rate, but it was an artificial gift. The level we were on at the time of the Exodus was not earned. In the intervening month of Iyar, we worked on our development. Like the wheat crop, we engaged in a process of maturing, of living up to the level we reached in Nissan. Now, in Sivan, we finally "fill our boots." We finally reach the heights we had tasted — all by ourselves. Our spiritual maturation finally matches our externally granted level. In the third month, we complete the third and final stage of the growth procedure, matching the second stage to the first.

Harmony of Three

Let us further explore the idea that in this third stage the inner forces are harmonious with the external forces. The zodiac sign for Sivan is *teumim*, "twins." The concept of twins might seem to relate to the number two. But *teumim* signifies more than two. *Teumim* comes from the same root as *mat'im*, "matching" or "complementing." Twins are not merely two people — they are two people who match, who are complementary. In Torah terms, this is represented by the number three: two people, plus the harmonious relationship.[4] The importance of the number three to this month is highlighted in the Gemara:

> A certain Galilean expounded in the presence of Rabbi Chisda: "Blessed is the Merciful One, Who gave a three-fold Torah [Torah, *Nevi'im*, and *Kesuvim*] to a threefold people [*Kohanim*, *Levi'im*, and *Yisraelim*] through a third-born [Moshe] on the third day of purification in the third month [Sivan]."
>
> (*Shabbos* 88a)

"The threefold thread will not easily snap" (Koheles 4:12).

This level of completion reached at stage three will also have a lasting power. The number three always indicates strength and stability. A chair requires a minimum of three legs to stand. *Chazakah*, the process of confirming doubtful ownership of land, requires three years to establish the owner's status. An ox is considered lethal and is killed after it has attacked on three occasions. Many bridges, and the Eiffel Tower in Paris, are constructed from triangular sections for maximum strength.

"One who sees wheat in a dream will see peace, as it says (Tehillim 147:14), 'He places peace in your borders; He satisfies you with the choicest wheat' " (Berachos 57a).

The harmony between internal and external forces in the third stage signals the achievement of perfection. The concepts of harmony and perfection are also linguistically related to each other. Another word for harmony is *shalom*, "peace." This is based on the word *shaleim*, meaning "complete" or "perfect." The harmony in man and nature at this time signals that completion and perfection have been attained.

Higher Purpose

In Sivan, *bikkurim*, the first ripe fruits of the season, are brought to the Beis HaMikdash. This is a highly significant gesture; the amount of effort that has been invested in the crops is immense, and to give the first rewards of these efforts to the *Kohen* is a great emotional self-sacrifice.

"On Atzeres [Shavuos], judgment is passed on the fruit of the trees..." (Rosh HaShanah 16a).

Giving *bikkurim* is not merely praiseworthy in itself; it reflects the entire year's activities. During the year, when man is involved in the lowly physical tasks of plowing, sowing, and harvesting, his life seems to lack spiritual purpose. By dedicating the first fruits of his labor in this way, man shows that all of his efforts to sustain himself in the physical world are only to enable him to further his relationship with Hashem.[5]

Perfect Kindness

We have already learned that Nissan initiated an order of *chesed*. *Sefiras ha'omer*, being a process of working on one's quality of *chesed*, continued this order. Shavuos, the climax of *sefiras ha'omer*, therefore represents the perfection of this quality. *Chesed* is the prime requirement for the proper approach to Torah.

The Holy One, blessed be He, said to Moshe: "The Torah is being given to you only in the merit of Avraham..."

(*Shemos Rabbah* 28:1)

Avraham was the epitome of the quality of *chesed*, and it was in his merit that we received the Torah. Torah has to be studied *liShmah*, "for its own sake." As we learned, Torah *liShmah* is a Torah of *chesed*. It requires one to negate one's own desires in the same way a performer of *chesed* looks at the needs of others and not at his own needs. Since this is a fundamental prerequisite for accepting the Torah, it is not surprising that we read the megillah of Rus at this time.

> Rabbi Zeira said: "This megillah contains no laws of what is pure or impure, of what is permitted or what is forbidden, so why was it written? To teach you the reward for those who bestow kindness."
>
> *(Rus Rabbah 2:14)*

The chesed of Rus has its origins in her ancestor Lot, who learned chesed from his uncle Avraham.

Rus teaches us lessons of kindness, of thinking about others. Despite her royal origins, she clung to her destitute mother-in-law, supporting her in every way. She honored the memory of her husband by performing *yibbum* with Bo'az to perpetuate his name. She even acted with kindness toward Hashem — by converting to Judaism, she gave Him "pleasure." Rus projects the message of *chesed,* teaching us the quality needed for accepting the Torah.[6]

The act of bestowing kindness is called "*gomel chesed*." The word *gomel*, which means in this context "to bestow," also means "to wean" or "to make independent." This is rather peculiar, since these two meanings of *gomel* are contradictory — one implies giving, and one implies the lack of giving. How are we to understand this?

Let us look again at the wheat crop. We have already seen that the wheat also teaches this lesson of *chesed*, in that the land gives of itself to the grain. At this time of year, the ears of grain have ripened. This means that they are complete and mature. They no longer need the parent stalk; they are ready to detach, either to be eaten or to propagate the next generation. The word used in the Torah for ripening is *gomel*.[7] The kernels of grain are independent; they have been weaned.

The Torah calls the camel gamal, "independent." It is independent in that it can last without water for as much as fifteen days in temperatures of thirty-five degrees centigrade (Rabbi Shamshon Raphael Hirsch on Bereishis 21:8). (It manages this through a variety of techniques, including its ability to tolerate a rise in its body temperature without needing to sweat.)

With this, the land has performed the greatest act of kindness. There is no greater kindness one can do for someone than help him become independent. To free someone from needing any more *chesed* is the greatest *chesed*. To give someone the means of earning an income on his own is the highest form of charity.[8]

This is also a measure of one's motivations in performing *chesed*. Sometimes one's generosity may be mixed with a need to be a "giver," to have others dependent on oneself. This is a great danger for teachers who must teach their students to think for themselves, and parents, who must at some stage "let go." To act with genuine *chesed*, one must focus exclusively on the requirements of the other person and grant him the independence he needs.

"The work of a Torah teacher is to make himself superfluous" (Rabbi Shamshon Raphael Hirsch on Shemos 27:20).

The Essence of Torah

Self-negation in favor of others is not only a prerequisite for proper Torah study; it is also the essence of Torah. When a prospective convert came to Hillel and asked him to explain the whole Torah in a nutshell, Hillel replied: "What is hateful to you, do not do to your friend; that is the whole Torah."[9] This seems to be an inadequate answer — how does it include the mitzvos between man and Hashem?

The answer is that "your friend" does not refer only to a person; it also refers to Hashem.[10] The Torah teaches man to think about his obligations both to Hashem and to his fellow man.

Every time we perform mitzvos, we are reinforcing a drive to think about others rather than about ourselves. If it is a mitzvah between man and Hashem, it causes us to concentrate on our duties to Him. If it is a mitzvah between our fellow men and ourselves, it encourages us to focus on the needs of others. The path of fulfilling the mitzvos between man and Hashem, and those between man and man, takes one away from self-centeredness and toward unity with Hashem and society.[11]

Kingship

Rus was the "mother of the king."[12] As the megillah notes, her descendant was David, the first and greatest in the Judean dynasty of kings.[13] David HaMelech passed away on Shavuos, and we can be sure he was born on Shavuos,[14] too, for Hashem ensures that the lives of *tzaddikim* are complete.[15]

"The heart of the king is the heart of the entire congregation of Israel..." (Rambam, Hilchos Melachim 3:6).

The Torah concept of *malchus*, "kingship," implies more than merely a king and his people. True *malchus* unites the individuals into a super-organism. It integrates all of the parts into a whole that is greater than the sum of the parts. The king organizes all of his subjects into their proper places, focusing them all toward a common goal. He enables the kingdom to achieve much more than the aggregate of their efforts could ever achieve had they been working separately.

In order for the *malchus* to achieve this goal, the

people must *live* for the *malchus*. This is especially true for the king, who must dedicate himself to the nation to the extent that he negates his own self entirely. He must possess the quality of *chesed*, utter dedication to the needs of others.

A Jewish king has an even more special task. He must also be a perfect medium to transmit Hashem's authority and kingship to the people. He must unreservedly devote himself to ensuring that the people fulfill the will of Hashem. David was the quintessential king, who lived entirely for his role in reflecting Hashem's authority onto the people.[16]

Dibbur, "speech," is the tool used in the creation and implementation of *malchus*. The kingdom is united, organized, and focused through instruction:

For the king's rule is with his word...

(Koheles 8:4)

The relay of words, in the form of instruction and guidance, enables the *malchus* to combine into a cohesive unit and accomplish its goals.

There is a powerful example in nature of *malchus* at its best. Bees form a complex society, headed by a queen. Each bee on its own has no individual existence and cannot function by itself. But collectively the hive survives and displays a remarkable intelligence. Different bees fulfill different roles — some collect pollen, some produce honey, others look after the young. Working together in a structured kingdom, they accomplish a complex goal. And what is the word for "bee" in the Torah? *Devorah*, with the same root as *dibbur!* For each bee is the "word" of the kingdom. They have no individual lives; they each live for the hive, serving as an instruction in the relay of the hive's

King David's dedication to his original job as shepherd proved his quality of chesed; kindness to animals is performed with no self-interest, for they do not repay favors (see Shemos Rabbah 2:2).

The word dabar, based on the word dibbur, means "leader," i.e., commander (Sanhedrin 8a and Rashi there).

workings. Their name captures the essence of their existence.

The bee is termed *devorah* for another reason. They possess an incredibly sophisticated form of communication that we would never expect to see in an insect. When a bee locates a new source of pollen, it reports this information to the other bees in the hive. Through a complex dance, it communicates not only the distance to the flower but also its direction relative to the sun! It does this inside the hive by converting the horizontal angle to the flower into a vertical angle on the honeycomb. Even cloudy days do not stop it, for it has the remarkable ability to determine the sun's position through the polarized light coming through the clouds. The name *devorah* captures the essence of its nature as an instruction of *malchus* and as a creature of communication.[17]

" 'These are the words [devarim] which Moshe spoke to all Israel...' (Devarim 1:1). Just as bees [devorah] follow the leadership of their queen, so do Yisrael follow the leadership of their tzaddikim and prophets" (Yalkut Shimoni 795).

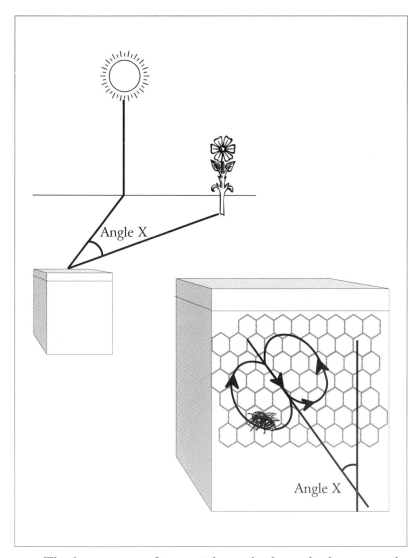

The bee traces a figure-eight path along the honeycomb. The angle of the straight section of this path against the vertical of the honeycomb equals the angle from the hive to the flower relative to the sun.

TAMUZ

Summer Heat

Wₑ are now approaching the height of summer. Eretz Yisrael, like all lands in the region, has fiercely hot summer months. The name *Tamuz* itself means "heat."[1] The blazing sun often raises the temperature to as much as 35° C. Being outdoors for extended periods can be dangerous; precious body fluid is lost to the heat, leading to dehydration.

The effects of the heat are clearly noticeable in nature. The green shoots of spring are now yellow and withered. The bubbling springs and brooks are drying up. The earth, formerly moist and productive, bakes under the scorching sun and begins to crack and fragment.

As we noted earlier in this work, the times of the year that bring extremes of environmental conditions are times of national hardship: the Seventeenth of Tamuz and Tishah B'Av in summer, and the Tenth of Teves in winter.[2] With an outlook that favors mediums over extremes, the Torah determines that the extreme temperatures at these times of year reflect an unfavorable situation for the Jewish people.

This period of summer hardship extends from the

beginning of Tamuz until halfway through Av. The entire month of Tamuz is governed by harsh judgment,[3] and the unfavorable nature of this period worsens with the arrival of the Seventeenth of Tamuz. It continues during the three-week period between the Seventeenth of Tamuz and Tishah B'Av, when it reaches its climax.[4]

On the Seventeenth of Tamuz, five tragedies occurred:[5]

- The first *luchos* (tablets) were broken by Moshe when he came down from Har Sinai and saw the people worshiping the golden calf.

- The *tamid* offering in the Beis HaMikdash was no longer brought.

- The walls of Yerushalayim were breached by Titus at the time of the second Beis HaMikdash.

- Apostemus, the wicked Roman commander, burned a Torah scroll in an attack on Jewish villages several years before the destruction of the second Beis HaMikdash.

- An idol was placed in the Sanctuary (some say by Apostemus).

Let us take a closer look at how this time of tragedy is manifest in nature.

Dryness and Desolation

Not only is the destruction of the Temples called *"churban,"* but this word is also used to describe barren wilderness and hot, dried-up land. The term is sometimes even used to describe both conditions simultaneously, one literally and one metaphorically:

For day and night Your Hand has been heavily upon me; my freshness has been transformed with the summer dryness [churvanei kayitz]...

(Tehillim 32:4)

Destruction is inherently associated with the concept of desolation, a barren and bleak land. As history has shown, the absence of the Jewish people in Eretz Yisrael has always been marked by the prevalence of physical desolation. In our absence, the land has never been fruitful or productive — it has been little more than a desert.

It is the lack of rain which turns the countryside into desert. Let us therefore explore the significance of rain and the withholding of it.

(Note that there is an important difference between these environmental conditions when they occur during summer and when they occur due to national punishment at times of the year when rain is expected. When they occur as punishment we pray that these conditions will cease and that there will be rain. But we do not pray for rain during the hot summer months. The harsh conditions of summer have become part of the yearly cycle; the mere presence of rain will not change summer into spring. The only solution will be at the time of Mashiach, when the cycle of seasons will be different in a way similar to conditions before the Flood, when it was spring all year long.[6])

Broken Connections

As we already learned, the relationship between heaven and earth is manifest on a physical level as rain. Thus, a healthy relationship between Hashem and the Jewish people is often described in terms of its manifestation in the rain, as we find in the Shema:

And it shall come to pass, if you listen to My mitzvos...that I shall give your land rain in its proper time, the early rains and the late rains...

(Devarim 11:13–14)

Conversely, an absence of rain indicates a breakdown in our relationship with Hashem:

Guard yourselves, lest you turn your hearts away...and Hashem's anger shall be kindled against you, and He shall stop up the heavens, and there shall be no rain...

(Ibid., 16–17)

When we turn away from Hashem, He prevents the rain from falling. The desired effect is to encourage our return to Him through fasting and prayer. In fact, the Talmudic tractate *Ta'anis*, which deals with fast days, does not center on the fasts of Yom Kippur and Tishah B'Av, as one might expect. These are left for the end. The main focus of the tractate is on fast days that have been instituted because of lack of rain.

The essence of a fast day is to reestablish our connection with Hashem, the breakage of which is signified by lack of rain. A fast day is to be occupied with repentance and prayer, expressing a desire to relate to Hashem and to redress our former lack of communication. This lack of communication, which is essentially a lack of connection, is seen as the cause for our hardships:

Because I was silent, my bones wasted away with my groaning. For day and night Your hand was heavily upon me; my moisture has been transformed with the summer dryness...

(Tehillim 32:3–4)

The word used for "silent," *hecherashti*, means more than just an absence of speech; it refers to a complete lack of communication. It is based on the word *cheresh,* which refers to a deaf-mute. It is also related to the word *cheres*, which refers to earthenware. Earthenware is baked clay, earth which can no longer absorb water. Which brings us full circle, for the suffering of these months is manifest in a dry, baked land, which cannot absorb water and has no interaction with the skies.

Isolation

The loss of connection between the skies and the land is not the only breakage that occurs at this time. The land itself breaks up. In the heat of summer, when there is no moisture, the land becomes brittle and begins to crack and fragment. It was the waters of winter that held the land together; without them, the soil loses its cohesiveness.

The implications of this are clear. The land represents the Jewish people. A loss of cohesiveness with Hashem goes hand in hand with a loss of cohesiveness within the Jewish people. One cannot reject Hashem and still unite with others, nor can one be dedicated to Hashem whilst isolated from relationships with other people. But why should this be?

Let us first explore the lack of connection with Hashem. One of the sins which brought about the destruction of the first Beis HaMikdash was idolatry; this was also at the root of the golden calf's construction. One may wonder what is so inherently evil about idolatry — surely it is just a foolish mistake, not actually evil. But idolatry, as the first prohibition on the two tablets, is a cardinal sin and the result of a powerful inner urge. What is the evil of this act and what is behind the drive to do it?

A monotheist knows that there is one God Who controls the universe and to Whom one is accountable. Faced with such a situation, his concerns focus on his obligations to this all-powerful Being. The idolater, on the other hand, focuses on the intermediaries Hashem uses in the functioning of this world. The constellations are all indicative of the flow of various spiritual forces. Each agent supplies a distinct power. The allure of focusing on the intermediaries can be compared to a shopping mall — there are a host of different suppliers for your needs from whom you can pick and choose. The deities are there to serve you, to fulfill your desires. You are not accountable to any of them. Idolatry is really the worship of the fulfillment of one's own desires.[7]

Hence, the root of idolatry, the source of separation from Hashem, is selfish desire. Accountability and obligations stand in the way of personal agendas and wishes. Seeking to escape from submission, the sinner turns to idolatry. By isolating himself from the Creator, he can focus on his own desires.[8]

The one who isolates himself seeks his own desires.
(Mishlei 18:1)

Isolation from other people is based on the same root. To fully integrate with other people, to create a true community, one must negate one's own desires and focus on the needs of others. One must dwell on obligations rather than on rights, on giving rather than on taking. Neglect of one's communal responsibilities is based on the pursuit of one's own desires. This lack of cohesiveness between people brought about baseless hatred, the cause of the destruction of the second Beis HaMikdash. Connection is called חבור (*chibbur*) in Hebrew. The break-up of *chibbur* is חרב (*charav*) — *churban*.

Eyes of the Owl

There is a chapter of Tehillim which describes the suffering in exile:

From the sound of my wailing, my bones have clung to my flesh. I am like a ka'as *of the desert; I have become as the* kos *of the barren wilderness [charavos].*

(Tehillim 102:6–7)

It is unclear which bird is referred to by the word *ka'as*.[9] But the *kos* would seem to be the little owl, *Athene noctua*, a small nocturnal predator that lives in ruins and other barren places.[10] This bird represents the themes of destruction we have explored. First, as the verse highlights, it lives in areas of *churban*, barren wilderness.[11] Being active in the cool of night, it can survive in areas devoid of water.[12] Night represents exile (see the section on Cheshvan). The little owl's cry is a long and mournful-sounding wail. It is also a lone bird that isolates itself

from other members of its species.

The Gemara notes that this bird has frontal eyes, like those of a human being.[13] Most birds have eyes situated on the sides of their heads, so they can be constantly on the lookout for predators. Having eyes at the sides of their heads gives them a much wider field of view and enables them to see approaching danger in almost any direction. The placement of the eyes demonstrates watchfulness and caution.

Owls, on the other hand, live at the very top of the food chain. There are no larger birds that prey on them. Their eyes are placed right at the front of their heads, facing forward, focused only on the food they pursue and consume. Their eyes are also extremely large, enabling them to detect their prey at considerable distances. The owl's eyes are therefore primarily instruments to aid in satisfying its hunger.

This expresses the problems discussed earlier. The sufferings of *churban* were caused at root by desire. Following their personal interests, the nation fell to idolatry, licentiousness, and hatred (in the respective eras). They disregarded the sinful nature and disastrous consequences of their actions. They were following their eyes, the instruments of desire:

> *...and do not follow after your hearts and after your eyes, after which you stray.*
>
> (Bemidbar 15:39)

The eye sees, the heart desires, and the body sins.

> (*Rashi* loc. cit.)

Sefer Yetzirah assigns a dominant ability to each month. Tamuz, it states, is associated with sight.

The misuse of the eyes is the first step toward desire, sin, and *churban*. And the root of all *churban* lies in the spies' evil report concerning Eretz Yisrael. During their mission, which took place during Tamuz and Av, they abused their task of using their eyes to see the land properly.[14] Instead of viewing the positive aspects of the land, they saw only negative aspects.

Sins of Fire

That the name *Tamuz* means "heat" does not only relate to the weather. It is also associated with the feelings a person experiences at this time. In Tamuz, people experience the flames of desire. It is this that can bring on sins such as idolatry.[15] In fact, Tamuz was an idol worshiped with fire.[16]

It is the sins committed in the heat of summer, the negative prohibitions that are transgressed out of the fires of desire, that are punished with the fires of Gehinnom.[17] This is alluded to in a verse which speaks about purifying the vessels captured in war:

> *Anything that came about through fire shall be passed through fire and become pure...*
>
> (Bemidbar 31:23)

It was these types of sin which were punished with the burning of the Beis HaMikdash. The sins committed in winter are of a different sort; we shall learn about them in "Teves."

The zodiac of this month is sartan, the crab (Cancer). Crabs are typically consumed by people who are overly concerned with consuming food of all types. As with the owl, we see the concept of desire (Shem MiShmuel, Tamuz 5672).

Fired Up

It may seem that all is doomed in Tamuz. But there is nothing in this world that is necessarily bad. The challenge of Tamuz is to use its heat and fire for the good. They can be utilized for growth in Torah, which is also called fire:

The Torah scholar who is fiery — it is the Torah that boils within him!

(Ta'anis 4a)

Although anger is usually a sign of evil, it means something else entirely when displayed by a Torah scholar.[18] It signifies the fiery spirit of one who does not let life wash over him in an emotional numbness, but who knows the truth of what life is all about and feels strongly about it. The fires of desire are thereby diverted to the fiery passion of Torah study.[19]

Furthermore, the fiery nature of Torah signifies its importance in conquering the divisive isolation that is the danger of Tamuz:

Why is the Torah compared to fire, as it is written, *"Surely my word is like fire,"* says Hashem (Yirmeyahu 23:29)? For just as one cannot create a fire out of a single [stick, but one must rub two sticks together], so, too, Torah is not established in a lone individual [but requires interactive discussion].

(Ta'anis 7a)

Even a month as potentially dangerous as Tamuz contains unique abilities for growth. One can passionately involve oneself in Torah and cause sparks of wisdom to fly out of heated arguments to discover the truth of Torah. If one resists the fires of desire, one can attain the fire of Torah:[20]

Hashem came from Sinai... From His right hand went forth a fiery law for them.

(Devarim 33:2)

LATE SUMMER

AV

Scorching Heat

The spring harvest has passed, high summer is finished, but we are not saved.

(Yirmeyahu 8:20, read in the haftarah on Tishah B'Av)

From the beginning of Av, we minimize joy...

(Ta'anis 26b)

The first weeks of Av are the most extreme part of summer. The heat of summer is building up to its most intense degree. The strength of the sun causes many to suffer from the pain of drought.

The period of hardship in Tamuz that we described intensifies with the onset of Av. The peak is reached on Tishah B'Av, "the Ninth of Av." The suffering of Tishah B'Av is rooted in an incident that took place in the desert nearly three and a half thousand years ago. Spies were sent out to survey Eretz Yisrael. They returned with reports of the fearsome nature of its inhabitants, stating that conquest would be impossible. The Jews wept bitterly, showing a lack of trust in Hashem, Who had brought them out of Mitzrayim and through the Reed Sea.

Rabbi Yochanan said: "That day was the eve of Tishah

"O Zion!...You were established in [the month of] Ziv to be a splendor, and you were destroyed with fury in the month of Av..." (Kinnos, "Tzion Yedidus").

B'Av. The Holy One, blessed is He, said, 'You are weeping for no reason. I shall establish this day for you as a time to weep for all generations.' "

(Ta'anis 29a)

The name of this month, Av (אב), is an acrostic of the powers who destroyed the two Temples: Edom (אדום) and Bavel (בבל).

Hashem decreed then that the Jews would not enter Eretz Yisrael for another forty years. Thus did the ninth of Av become predestined for misfortune. The first Beis HaMikdash was destroyed on this day, beginning the Babylonian exile. The second Beis HaMikdash was destroyed on this day, beginning the exile of Edom. Bar Kochba's stronghold in the city of Beitar was captured on this day. Yerushalayim was razed to the ground by Turnus Rufus on this day. The decree of the Spanish expulsion was signed on this day. The First World War began on Tishah B'Av. The trains started transporting Jews to the gas chambers on Tishah B'Av.

A terrible day, indeed. Yet the very singularity of this day has served as an inspiration to many. At the time of the Spanish expulsion in particular, the fact that the decree was signed on Tishah B'Av helped many to recognize events as clearly being controlled by Hashem. And just as it was Hashem who was punishing them, it would be Hashem who would one day rescue them.

"How do we know that the second Beis HaMikdash was destroyed on the Ninth of Av? As we have learned, good things are brought about on worthy days, and bad things are brought about on bad days" (Ta'anis 29a).

On this night, the calendrical cycle turned to an inauspicious date...

(Kinnos, "B'Leil Zeh")

Tishah B'Av stands as the ultimate proof of our concept of time. Time is truly cyclical, with Tishah B'Av being, not a one-time day of sorrow, but a day which is predestined annually for hardship.

The Power of the Lion

The lion [aryeh] roars, and who shall not be afraid?

(Amos 3:8)

The Beis HaMikdash is called *"aryeh,"* as it says, *Ariel...* (Yeshayah 29:1).

The kingship of David is called *"aryeh,"* as it says, *What a lioness was your mother; she crouched between the lions...* (Yechezkel 19:2).

"The lion has six names: ari, because everyone is afraid [misyare'in] of it; kefir, because anyone who sees it denies [kofer] any chance of survival; lavi, because it snatches the hearts [levavos] of people; layish, because the flesh of people is as nothing [lo yesh] in its maw; shachal, because everyone is terrified [shochel] of it; and shachatz, because it tears [mashchitz] with its teeth" (Midrash Mishlei 20:2).

Yisrael is called "*aryeh*," as it says, *Yehudah is a young lion...* (Bereishis 49:9).

And Nevuchadnetzar is called "*aryeh*," as it says, *The lion arose from his thicket* (Yirmeyahu 4:7).

(*Shemos Rabbah 29*)

" 'Therefore the lion of the forest has struck them...' (Yirmeyahu 5:6) — this refers to Babylon" (Vayikra Rabbah 13:5).

The first dynasty of Davidic kingship came crashing down when Babylon, under the reign of the wicked Nevuchadnetzar, destroyed the Beis HaMikdash and sent the nation into exile. The Babylonian exile was the first of the four exiles to which we have been subjected. It is paralleled by the lion, the first of the creatures to appear in Daniel's vision:

I saw in my vision at night... Four great beasts came up from the sea... The first was like a lion...

(Daniel 7:2–4)

"The lion is the mightiest of the animals and turns away before no one" (Mishlei 30:30).

The lion is called the king of beasts, and justly so. Weighing up to five hundred pounds, these powerful felines are right at the top of the food chain. They will attack even larger animals, and there have been many instances of people falling prey to them. Lions were common in Israel until around a thousand years ago.

"...I will bring evil from the north and great destruction. The lion arose from his thicket, and the destroyer of nations is on his way; he has gone out of his place to make your land desolate; he shall lay your cities waste, without inhabitants" (Yirmeyahu 4:6–7).

As we noted earlier, the most favorable times of year for us are the temperate months of Nissan and Tishrei, and it is then that we celebrate Pesach and Sukkos. The theme of Av, on the other hand, is extremes. In the extreme heat of summer, the tables are turned. Foreign powers which revel in such extremes become a threat. Empires rise to their zenith and turn against us. The mighty Nevuchadnetzar triumphed in this month and destroyed the Beis HaMikdash. All of this is reflected in the extreme power of the lion, this month's constellation.[1]

Hashem says: "With that which I punish, I heal... They

sinned with lions, as it is written, *Her princes in the midst of her are as roaring lions [in their terrorization of the people]* (Tzefaniah 3:3); they were punished with lions: *The lion [Nevuchadnetzar] arose from his thicket...* (Yirmeyahu 4:7); and they shall be comforted with lions: *The lion shall eat straw like an ox* (Yeshayahu 11:7).

(Pesikta Rabbasi 33)

The Lion King

The lion represents Bavel, the power that destroyed the first Beis HaMikdash. But the might of the lion has its positive uses, too.

Rabbi Yehudah ben Teimah said: "Be as mighty as a lion...to fulfill the will of your Father in Heaven."

(Avos 5:24)

This is not a general statement. The might of the lion has a particular application in the service of Hashem. It is this strength that is required in the fight against sin. The powerful urges of the evil inclination cannot be defeated by Torah knowledge alone; it requires a tremendous inner strength.

"A man should strengthen himself like a lion to rise in the morning for the service of the Creator" (Shulchan Aruch 1:1).

Who is mighty? He who conquers his [evil] inclination....

(Ibid. 4:1)

Furthermore, as we saw in the *midrash* cited earlier, the lion, king of beasts, also represents the majesty of the Davidic kingship and the Beis HaMikdash. Mashiach ben David, who will herald the final redemption, will be born on Tishah B'Av.[2] From the very place of despair comes the source of salvation. The lion displays the royalty that is the legacy of David's ancestor Yehudah.

Yehudah is the young lion...

(Bereishis 49:9)

Call of the Camel

In the list of the four creatures that possess only one of the two signs needed to be kosher, the camel is mentioned first. It parallels Bavel, the first exile.

> The camel [*gamal*] is Bavel, as it says, [*Daughter of Bavel, condemned to devastation,*] *happy is he who shall pay you your recompense* [*gemulecha*] *for all that you bestowed* [*gamalta*] *upon us* (Tehillim 137:8).
>
> (*Vayikra Rabbah* 13:5)

This Midrash notes some parallels:

- Just as the camel is *ma'aleih geirah*, "raises up its cud," so did Bavel raise up its voice in praise of Hashem: "Now I, Nevuchadnetzar, praise and exalt and honor the King of Heaven..."[3]

- Just as the camel brings up its cud, so did Bavel "bring up" (i.e., form an environment in which were

created) *tzaddikim*, such as Daniel.

- The camel is *ma'aleih geirah*. So, too, Bavel dragged along (*megarer*, based on the word *geirah*) another kingdom after it — Persia and Media.

The camel parallels the exile of Bavel in other ways, too. As a creature suited to hot, arid conditions, it matches the heat of the summer. Additionally, we find the following statement about the camel:

> The camel says, ...*Hashem shall roar from on high, He shall utter His voice from His holy abode, He shall roar mightily on account of His abode* (Yirmeyahu 25:30).
>
> (*Perek Shirah*)

Most animals stalk silently toward their prey before attacking. When a camel becomes angry, it bays a guttural roar before it lashes out with its large hooves. This advance warning gives one time to beat a hasty retreat (provided one has suitable reflexes).[4]

In the same way, Hashem's decree that Bavel would destroy the Beis HaMikdash did not come without warning.[5] The prophets urged the people to repent from their sinful ways. Unfortunately, the people did not heed the warnings, and Bavel attacked.

" 'And because He loved your forefathers, He chose their seed after them, and He brought you out...to drive out nations greater and mightier than you from before you, to bring you in, to give you their land as an inheritance...' (Devarim 4:37–38) — as a man who drives out the camels from the field and brings in the sheep" (Midrash Lekach Tov loc. cit.).

We noted in "Sivan" that the name gamal means "independent," signifying the camel's independence from water. Perhaps this relates to the sin of the Jewish people which brought on the evil of Bavel. The desire to be independent from Hashem is the root of idolatry, which was the sin that caused the first destruction.

Sour Grapes

> *Moshe sent them to spy out the land of Cana'an...and it was the days of the first ripe grapes...*
>
> (Bemidbar 13:17, 20)

The spies were sent out at the end of Sivan,[6] but the Torah tells us when they were sent in relation to the grape harvest. The ripening of the first grapes, which occurs over the months of Tamuz and Av, reflects the potential dangers of this period.[7]

Vines are unusual in that they must be supported, usually on (dead) wooden sticks. Similarly, the Jewish people are supported on the merit of their deceased forefathers (Vayikra Rabbah 36:2; Midrash Shmuel 16:1).

The Jewish people are likened to the vine in many ways:

- Just as the vine requires much tending to grow well, so do the Jewish people require Torah study and mitzvos to grow spiritually.[8]

- Just as the vine requires good soil for its optimal growth, so do the Jewish people require Eretz Yisrael for their optimal growth.[9]

- Just as the vine grows to the height of that which supports it, so do the Jewish people grow in accordance with their Torah study, which supports them.[10]

- Just as vines are planted in rows rather than haphazardly, so did the Jewish people camp in a special arrangement in the desert.[11]

- Just as grapes are trodden upon but then become wine on the tables of kings, so are the Jewish people downtrodden in this world but will eventually rise above all other nations.[12]

We will focus on the first ripening of the grapes that takes place at this time. This important event is spoken of as being representative of the history of the Jewish people:

My beloved had a vineyard in a fertile hill; he dug it, and cleared away its stones, and planted it with the choicest vine, and built a tower in the midst of it, and hewed out a wine vat in it. He hoped it would produce good grapes, but it produced sour grapes. And now, O dweller of Jerusalem and man of Yehudah, please judge between me and my vineyard. What more could I have done to my vineyard that I had not done for it? Why was it that when I hoped for it to produce good grapes, it produced sour grapes? And now, I will tell you what I will do to my vineyard: I will remove its hedge, and it shall be eaten up; and break down its wall, and it shall be trodden upon; and I will lay it waste. It shall not be pruned or hoed, and briars and thorns will come up; I will also command the clouds, that they shall not rain on it. For the House of Yisrael is the vineyard of Hashem of hosts...

(Yeshayahu 5:1–7)

Enormous effort is invested in a vineyard. It requires careful preparation of soil, strong fences, and vigilant guarding. Yet, even after all this work, a good vintage is not certain. There is always a risk that the grapes will be sour. Although the owner might try to plant the choicest red vine, the seeds he plants do not always possess the traits of their parent vine. There is always a chance that sour grapes will be produced.

"How did You concentrate in Your anger to devastate Your vineyard at the hand of the vandalizing villain?..." (Kinnos, "Eichah Atzta").

This, unfortunately, was the case with the Jewish people.[13] Hashem provided the finest land for us, and He gave us the Torah to protect us from harmful influences. But for all this effort, we sometimes did not turn out according to His desire. We were "sour" with sinful deeds. In His disappointment, Hashem tore down the fences to allow the wild animals, the evil nations of the

world, to consume us, as Yerushalayim burned:

"O Zion, lament over your house which is burnt; cry out bitterly over the ruination of your vines..." (Kinnos, "Tzion Tekoneini").

Therefore, so says Hashem the Lord: "As the vine among the trees of the forest, which I have given to the fire to consume, so I have given the residents of Yerushalayim."

(Yechezkel 15:6)

Yet if at least some of the grapes on the vine are good, then the vineyard owner will perhaps not destroy the vineyard in frustration. So too, we pray that Hashem looks to the merit of the righteous people among us and has mercy on us for their sake:[14]

"Wine was created only to comfort mourners..." (Eiruvin 65a).

Return, please, Hashem of legions; look down from heaven and see, and show concern for this vine...

(Tehillim 80:15)

Boar of the Forest

When the vineyard is laid open to the wild beasts, it falls victim to one animal in particular:

You caused a vine to journey out of Egypt... Why have you broken down its fences, so that wayfarers pluck its fruit? The boar of the forest destroys it...

(Tehillim 80:9–14)

The boar of the forest — this refers to the wicked Eisav...

(Midrash Shmuel 16)

"[Jerusalem] has fallen... Those boar of the forest jeered, 'Where are her pious ones?' ...And Zion spread her hands [in despair]" (Kinnos, "Shavas Suru").

The wild boar, and its domestic variety, the pig, parallels Eisav and the kingdom of Edom (Rome). It is to this evil empire that the second Beis HaMikdash fell, launching the fourth exile, which continues today.

The wild boar, regarded as a destructive animal by the Torah, enjoys a similar lack of popularity today. Still very common in the Galil, Golan, and Carmel regions of Israel, these creatures weigh up to 250 pounds and possess tusks up to 10 inches long. Noisy, short-tempered, and messy, they frequently raid orchards, leaving a trail of devastation in their wake. On rare occasions they have been known to injure and even kill people.

The first time the Midrash draws a parallel to Edom is in its list of the non-kosher species of animals. The pig, fourth in the list, possessing split hooves but not chewing its cud, parallels the fourth kingdom, Edom. The Midrash details some of these comparisons:[15]

- Unlike other animals, which fold their legs underneath their bodies when crouching, the pig stretches out its legs in front of it. In doing so, it is advertising its one and only kosher sign, pretending that it is a kosher animal. Similarly, the kingdom of Edom commits all manners of atrocities, but still proclaims itself to be a cultured advocate of truth and justice. Any perceptive and objective observer of modern history will have noticed this phenomenon on many occasions. (Edom's pretense at being kosher is further discussed in "Adar.")

- Just as the pig does not raise up its cud, so too, Edom does not raise up praise to Hashem. Edom rejects Hashem's authority, as will be further discussed in the next subsection.

- Just as the pig does not bring up its cud, so does Edom not "bring up" (i.e., support) *tzaddikim*. Worse, they kill them. The slaughter of Rabbi Akiva and other Sages are typical examples.

- Unlike the camel, hyrax, and hare, the pig is not *ma'aleih geirah* — it does not bring up its cud. So, too, unlike the other kingdoms, Edom does not drag

"When the Hasmonean kings were vying for power, Aristobulus was inside Yerushalayim and Hyrkenus was on the outside. Every day, they would lower [from the walls] a box of coins with a rope, and the others would raise up tamid sacrifices. There was an old man present who was well versed in Greek. He called to them in Greek, 'As long as they are busy serving Hashem, they cannot be delivered into your hands!' The next day, when they lowered the box of money, the others sent up a pig. When it reached halfway up the wall, it dug its hooves in, and Eretz Yisrael shook for a distance of four hundred parsah. At that time, they said, 'Cursed is he who raises pigs, and cursed is he who teaches his son Greek' " (Sotah 49b).

along (*megarer*, based on the word *geirah*) another evil kingdom after it. At the end of *galus Edom*, Mashiach will arrive.

The Pig-Headed Pig

Pigs are unusual creatures in that they have virtually no neck. Their massive skulls grow almost directly out of their shoulders. This means that they have very little mobility of the head.

The significance of this relates to the following verse:

> *Lift up your eyes upon high and perceive Who created these!*
> (Yeshayahu 40:26)

As we noted in the Introduction, this is an instruction to lift up our heads and be awed by the majesty of the cosmos. Humbled by the vastness of the universe, awed at the dynamics of the galaxy, man submits himself to Hashem's authority.

The pig, with its short neck, cannot lift up its head to contemplate the skies. As such, it represents Edom, who does not accept the lesson the skies are trying to teach us:[16]

> *The pig* refers to Edom... Not only does he not praise Hashem, but he curses and abuses Him, saying "Who is there for me in the heavens?
> (*Vayikra Rabbah* 13:5)

The wicked reign of Edom has lasted for two thousand years. We pray for the end of this exile, for the fulfillment of Hashem's promise:

> *And I shall banish the terrible beast from the land...*
> (Vayikra 26:6)

The terrible beast means none other than the pig...the wicked Eisav.

(*Midrash Tehillim* 120:6)

The Solitary Widow

Alas, she sits in solitude. The city that was great with people has become like a widow.

(Eichah 1:1)

The relationship between Hashem and the Jewish people is now at its weakest. In the fierce summer heat, the land has become utterly dry, lacking any moisture. Separated from the husbandry of the rains, the land has become like a solitary widow.

> " '...She has become like a widow' — Rabbi Yehudah said: 'This is a blessing. She is like a widow, but not actually a widow; she is like a woman whose husband has gone abroad but intends to return' " (*Ta'anis* 20a).

The separation of the land from the sky and the fragmentation of the land are at their greatest. It is at this time that the threat of *galus*, "dispersion," became a reality. For when the Jewish people separate themselves from Hashem and from internal unity, Hashem in turn separates and disperses them from the land and from each other. The unity between Hashem and the Jewish people that was achieved during Sivan has been shattered:

At that time, through our sins, the Mikdash was destroyed... The constellation of the twins appeared separated...

(*Kinnos, "Ad Ana Bichyah"*)

There Is Hope

This is a time to mourn. But it is not a time to despair. "Absence makes the heart grow fonder." We can strengthen ourselves at this time of separation and yearn for the reestablishment of the bonds that have been broken. The act of mourning itself demonstrates that one feels for the nation's plight. Our lives now are relatively comfortable, so when we gather together to mourn for those who suffered millennia ago, it shows we are concerned for others after all. Personal desire would lead us to satisfy our hunger, but we fast in acknowledgment of our duties to Hashem and to the Jewish people. That is the path toward healing the ills of Tishah B'Av.

"Whoever suffers along with the community merits to see the comforting of the community" (Ta'anis 11a).

> Whoever mourns over Yerushalayim merits to witness its joy!
>
> *(Ta'anis 30b)*

This bonding we engage in on Tishah B'Av will cause this day of sorrow to become a day of connection between Hashem and ourselves, the rendezvous of *mo'ed*:

> *So says Hashem of hosts: "The fast of the fourth [month, the Seventeenth of Tamuz], the fast of the fifth [the Ninth of Av], the fast of the seventh [Tzom Gedalyah], and the fast of the tenth [the Tenth of Teves] shall be for the house of Yehudah as gladness and joy and good mo'adim..."*
>
> *(Zechariah 8:19)*

Midway Change

On the fifteenth of Av, an abrupt change takes place. The season of suffering we have been in since the beginning of Tamuz comes to an end. It is replaced by a season of joy and launched by a quasi-festival:

> Rabban Shimon ben Gamliel said: "There were never festivals for Yisrael like the Fifteenth of Av and Yom Kippur, on which the maidens of Yerushalayim would go out dressed in garments of white... They would go out and dance in circles in the vineyards, and what would they say? 'Young men, lift your eyes, and consider who you

will select [for a wife]; pay no attention to beauty, but rather to lineage...' "

(Ta'anis 26b)

But what was the basis for such celebrations? The Gemara[17] gives several reasons for the joy of this day:

- On this day many thousands of years ago, the tribes of Yisrael were granted permission to marry into each other.

- Many years later on this date, the tribe of Binyamin, which had been excluded from the rest of the Jewish people due to the incident of the concubine at Givah,[18] were allowed once again to marry into the rest of the nation.

- It was on this day, forty years after the Jewish people's sin of crying over the spies' reports about Eretz Yisrael, that they realized that the decree of death had ceased.

- The wicked king of Yisrael, Yeravam, had placed sentries on the roads to prevent people from ascending to Yerushalayim for the festivals. On this date, King Hoshea annulled their authority.

- After a long period, the Romans finally allowed the victims of the massacre at Beitar to be given over for burial on this day.

- On this date, the work of cutting wood for the pyre on the altar would halt. Since the sun's strength begins to wane significantly at approximately this time, the wood would not dry out properly, possibly leaving worms inside which render the wood unfit for use. The release from this work enabled people to spend more time studying Torah (an activity particularly suited to the now lengthening nights[19]) and was thus a cause for celebration.

These seemingly disparate and somewhat cryptic reasons conceal a deeper pattern. Let us further explore this new stage in the cycle of the year.

Courtship

The key to understanding this time is in the seasonal change of the waning of summer noted in the last reason above. We have explored the pattern of the cycle of life that takes place during the course of the year. Nissan, in spring, began the process with renewal and rebirth. Maturity was reached in Sivan. Since then, we have been through the difficult stages of late summer. But now, as the nights grow longer and the days grow cooler, there is hope in sight. Soon the rainy season will begin, bringing new life to the parched ground. We already learned that rain is the "husband" of the land, the physical manifestation of the relationship between Hashem and the Jewish people. The fertilization of the land by the rains mirrors the consummation of the relationship between our Creator and us.

"From this day on, one who adds on [from the night hours to his Torah study] will have [days] added on [to his life]; one who does not add on [from the night hours to his Torah study] will be gathered in [before his time]" (Ta'anis 31a).[20]

Now is the time when we begin to prepare for that relationship. On Hashem's part, He acts toward us with endearment. The various tragedies and tribulations we were subjected to ceased. For our part, we celebrate the increase of our Torah studies. Torah is the medium for our relationship with Hashem, the means by which our souls connect with the Infinite.

Tu B'Av, when the sun's strength begins to wane and the rains are in sight, is a day which is ripe to prepare for relationships. That is why the Jewish people were granted permission to intermarry on this day. That is why the members of the tribe of Binyamin were permitted to intermarry on this day. And that is the reason why the maidens of Yerushalayim would go out to be matched to their partners on this day.

The dance of the maidens represents the mystical nature of the day. The maidens represent the Jewish people. The white garments that the maidens wore were symbolic of the purity attained on this day. The garments were lent out — even if the Jewish people are lacking in merit, Hashem grants them merit. The word for the circles in which they would dance, *machol*, is related to the word *mechilah*, "forgiveness."[21]

The process of endearment has begun. But for the relationship to grow, we must wait for the next month — Elul.

ELUL

Moving Closer

אני לדודי ודודי לי...

I am for my Beloved, and my Beloved is for me...
(Shir HaShirim 6:3)

The month of Elul marks a time of intense longing between Hashem and the Jewish people. It was during this time of closeness that Moshe ascended Har Sinai for the second time to receive the second set of tablets. Despite the terrible sin of the golden calf, Moshe was able to attain forgiveness on behalf of the Jewish people. The love Hashem has for us triumphed, and our relationship was renewed.

Since then, Elul has denoted a time of closeness, a time to move toward our Creator. This month is designated for *teshuvah*, which is often translated as "repentance" but literally means "return." With the *teshuvah* of Elul, we begin the process of returning to our Source, our Creator, a process that reaches its climax on Yom Kippur, the Day of Atonement.

Returning to the Source

The idea behind *teshuvah* is that it is a return to one's Source. In nature, too, we are following a return to the source at this time. For the last few months, we have been focusing on what came out of the ground, on the crops and fruit. Now our perspective returns to the ground itself. We now concentrate on plowing and preparing the soil. Soon the plants themselves will return to their source, as their seeds are buried in the earth that produced them. Stripped of the external attachments of shoots and leaves, the seeds — which are the bare essence of the plants — return to their source.

This is the concept of *teshuvah*. The blast of the shofar commands us to strip away from ourselves all excuses and all pretenses. We take a good long look at what we really are. Stripped down to the essence, we are ready to return to our Source, to stand before our Creator. Standing in such a position, we will feel a resolve, a responsibility, to improve in our thoughts and deeds.[1]

Preparing to Bestow

The natural indicator of all this is the approaching rains. The nights have been growing steadily longer, the temperatures have been cooling, and it is only a matter of weeks before the rains will return, bringing new life to the earth. Unfortunately, our urban lifestyles render us relatively insensitive to the magnitude of this process. It is important, though, to be aware that the rains that fall during this time are absolutely vital to the natural world in general and to man specifically.

In our conceptual terms of the rain being the "husband" of the land, this is the time when the husband is preparing to relate to his wife. We, as the earth, represent the female dimension in the stage prior to the consummation of the relationship. Thus, the *mazal* of Elul is the *besulah*, the maiden who has not yet united with her husband.

But the process of relating to Hashem requires work on our part. First, "I am for my Beloved," and only then is "my Beloved for me."[2] Hashem waits for us to make the first move.

"Return to Me, and I shall return to you..." (Malachi 3:7).

> *Return, O maiden of Israel!*
>
> (Yirmeyahu 31:20)

Preparing to Receive

The spiritual work of Elul is to return to Hashem through repentance and to reestablish our relationship with Him. How is this expressed in nature?

Let us review the state of separation from Hashem which we have experienced in the past months. We learned that the problem was manifest in the lack of connection between the land and the heavens. The lack of rain represented a break in the precious relationship between us.

But even if Hashem were to grant us rain now, it would be of no help. For the land has been baked hard and cannot absorb water. Any rain would simply accumulate on the surface of the land and cause flooding — another type of destruction. At the moment, the land is in an uncommunicative state. We noted that this was termed a state of *cheresh*, the term used to describe a deaf-mute, someone incapable of communication.

Because I was silent [hecherashti]...my freshness has been transformed with the summer dryness...

(Tehillim 32:3–4)

How do we take the land out of this state? How do we enable it to "relate" to the skies by absorbing the rains? Through plowing.

Does the one who plows do so forever in order to sow [without ever actually sowing] when he opens up and smoothes the land?

(Yeshayahu 28:24)

There are several types of plowing. The first type opens up the ground and enables it to absorb the forthcoming rains. The word for "plow" in the Torah is *choresh*. Here we have a case in which the verb is the opposite of the noun. We are *choresh* the land to take it out of its *cheresh* state. (A similar linguistic concept in Hebrew can be seen in the word *shoresh*, which as a noun means "root" and as a verb means "to uproot.") We open up the land to rain, and thereby take it out of its state of uncommunicativeness.[3] Through the process of plowing, we are preparing on a physical level for the forthcoming relationship with Hashem.

Breaking Through

There is another important aspect to the process of plowing. The hard land needs to be broken up in order to let the seed develop and grow. We smash through the restricting solidity of the earth.[4]

In the same way, earthliness is an obstruction to spiritual growth. The materialism of this world blocks one from fully developing. One method Hashem uses to free us from the bonds of materialism is suffering and exile. But there is another path, too — the *teshuvah* of Elul. Elul is the time to break out of the material involvement of one's lifestyle and to allow the seeds of spiritual growth to germinate.

The Need to Relate

These are the generations of the heavens and the earth...and no plant of the field was yet in the earth, and no herb of the field had yet grown, for Hashem our God had not caused it to rain on the earth, and there was no man to till the ground.

(Bereishis 2:4–5)

Why had Hashem not yet caused it to rain? Because there was no man to till the earth and to recognize the beneficence of the rains. When Adam arrived and recognized that they were essential for the world, he prayed for them, and they fell, and the trees and grasses sprouted.

(*Rashi*, citing *Chullin* 60b)

The spiritual work of Elul is very much rooted in the physical. It is because we recognize that the rains are so essential to our well-being that we turn to Hashem in prayer. And this is the whole point of the dry versus rainy seasons — the contrast encourages us to relate to Hashem. The hardship of drought and the need for a good crop are designed to encourage us to return to Hashem in heartfelt prayer, to beseech Him to bestow His grace upon us in the form of rain.

Elul is therefore a month in which *tefillah*, "prayer," plays an extremely significant role.[5] This itself gives us insights into the nature of prayer. It is also a statement of our role vis-à-vis Hashem — He is the Giver and we are the receivers. Our needs are in His Hands. This recognition is one of the ways in which prayer works. There is a famous question asked about prayer: How can we change Hashem's mind? Surely if we deserve it, He will give us what we ask for anyway; and if we do not deserve it, what good will it do to ask for it? The answer is that we are not changing Hashem's mind when we ask for things. Rather, by acknowledging that it is He who provides for our needs, we are making ourselves worthy of having our prayers answered.[6] By recognizing that it is Hashem who provides the rain, we are attaining a level whereby we are worthy of receiving rain.

Advance and Withdrawal

Each month corresponds spiritually to the month which is on the opposite side of the year to it. More specifically, the six summer months correspond to the six winter months. Nissan corresponds to Tishrei, Iyar to Cheshvan, Sivan to Kislev, and so on. In each of these pairs, the same elements are present, but in a different way, reflecting the difference between summer and winter. Nissan is the beginning of the year for kindness, while Tishrei begins the year for judgment. Sivan celebrates the giving of the Written Torah, while Kislev marks the victory of the Oral Torah over Greek philosophy. (This pattern is illustrated at the back of the book in "Time Cycle Two: The Symmetry of the Year.")

"Seedtime and harvest, Cold and heat, Summer and winter..." (Bereishis 8:22).

Elul's partner is Adar. Both of these months are preludes to the year's beginning. Elul is the prelude to the New Year for judgment. This is the strict process of Rosh HaShanah and Yom Kippur in the spiritual realm and the variable winter rains in the physical realm.

Adar is the prelude to the New Year for kindness — the miracles of Pesach and the beneficence of the summer dew. Both of these months are a time for *teshuvah*, but in very different ways. Since Elul precedes Hashem's judgment, it is conducive to *teshuvah miyirah*, repentance from awe. Adar, which precedes Hashem's kindness, is conducive to *teshuvah mei'ahavah*, repentance out of love.

To fully understand these two processes, we must examine and contrast nature at these times of year. In Adar, spring is just beginning. Plants are bursting out of the ground, spreading upward and outward. It is a time of expansiveness. In Elul, on the other hand, the reverse is taking place. The plants are decomposing, and the seeds will be returned to the earth. Everything is withdrawing, regressing, contracting.

This is the difference between repentance from love and repentance from fear. Repentance from love causes one to move out toward Hashem. It is a mood of expansiveness, free from restrictive fears. Repentance from awe has the opposite effect. In awe of Hashem's might, one withdraws fearfully.

זרע

FALL SEEDTIME

TISHREI

New Year

> The first of Tishrei is the new year for [the counting of] years, for the sabbatical years and the jubilee years, for the planting [of trees], and for the vegetables.
>
> (*Rosh HaShanah* 2a)

> Today is the birthday [literally, "conception"] of the world.
>
> (*Mussaf* prayer of Rosh HaShanah)

The first of Tishrei, the day on which man was created, begins the new year for the world. Unlike the first of Nissan, which is specifically the New Year for the cycle of spiritual development of the Jewish people, the first of Tishrei is the New Year for more worldly matters, and as such the day is significant for all mankind. The status of Tishrei as Rosh HaShanah for the physical world is clearly expressed in the laws of the *mishnah* cited above, all of which refer to agricultural situations. Additionally, Tishrei is the seventh month (from Nissan, the "head of the months"), and seven always represents the physical world, which was created in seven days.

The word tishrei actually means "fall." It is based on the word hasharah, "falling off," which is used to refer to leaves falling off trees in autumn.

Tishrei begins the season of *zera*, "fall seedtime." The sowing of seeds is the conception of the year for the plant kingdom. The simple act of sowing seeds contains a wealth of meaning, some facets of which we shall be exploring in the following pages.

Creation

> Hashem says: "Since you have entered for judgment before Me on Rosh HaShanah and have exited in peace, I consider it as though you are a new creation."
>
> (*Yerushalmi, Rosh HaShanah* 4:8)

The crops now begin a new cycle of life. This year's crops are not last year's — they are a new creation. The same is true of man. Rosh HaShanah is the day on which man was created, and it is the day on which man is recreated, every year.

This is not a cute idea based on an appealing parallel in nature. It is a very real fact. The greatest illustration of this comes from the history of Chanoch, in what is perhaps one of the most mysterious verses in the Torah:

> *Chanoch walked with God, and he was no more, for God took him away.*
>
> (Bereishis 5:24)

Chanoch was perfect, free of sin. Hashem did not want him to be affected by the wicked people of his time. But since he had no sins, he did not deserve to die. And, astonishingly, he did not die, as such. He simply was not here anymore. The Midrash explains that this happened on Rosh HaShanah.[1] The significance of this is as we have stated, that man is recreated on Rosh HaShanah. Chanoch did not die in the normal sense of the term. He was just not recreated on Rosh HaShanah when everyone else was.

The Conception of the Year

It is now, at the beginning of the year, that the itinerary for the coming year is set. The goals for mankind to reach in the coming year are designated, and the situations in life of the participants are assigned. The future has not been finalized, but the key elements are put into place. Rosh HaShanah is a day of all-inclusiveness; the rest of the year is an unfolding of the contents of Rosh HaShanah.

Why does it function this way? The answer is related to our explanation of how time warps in Nissan. In the higher worlds, the dimension of time does not exist. We might speak of them as "eternal," but they are really outside time altogether. The coming year does not exist there as a continuum of time, but as a single unit.

Rosh HaShanah is the interface. The program for the coming year unfolds through the higher worlds and arrives in our world on Rosh HaShanah. Since it is coming from a timeless dimension, it arrives in a timeless form — an integrated, all-inclusive blueprint for the year. Gradually, it will unfold to create the coming year.[2]

The parallel of this in nature is breathtaking. The seeds we now sow in the ground contain the *entire plant*. Every single aspect of the plant, from the shape of its leaves to the taste of its fruit, is encoded within the tiny seed. The entire future history of the plant has been encapsulated at this single point in time, in this small seed. All that remains to take place is the actualization of the blueprint, the gradual unfolding of the plans.

This is also true of a human being. The tiny speck

of genetic code that forms the fetus is a complete blueprint for the adult body at every stage of life.

This has powerful implications for the way in which we should live during Rosh HaShanah. We are laying the foundations for the entire year to come. Change is always possible, but it will be much more difficult later on. Now is the time to set the tone for the year ahead. It is essential to use this opportunity for spiritual growth.

Cleansing and Ingathering

...In the seventh month, on the tenth day of the month, you shall inflict your souls...for on this day He will cleanse you, to purify you from all your sins...

(Vayikra 16:29–30)

Following Rosh HaShanah and preceding Sukkos is Yom Kippur. To gain an understanding of this transition period, let us look at the *midrash* which discusses Yaakov's fear of being exposed when he impersonated his brother, Eisav, to receive the blessings:

Yaakov said to Rivkah, his mother, "But Eisav my brother is a hairy man, and I am smooth-skinned."

(Bereishis 27:11)

Rabbi Levi said: It is comparable to a hairy man and a bald man who stand at the entrance of a threshing floor. The husk is blown onto the hairy man, and it becomes stuck in his hair. The husk is blown onto the bald man, and he reaches up with his hand and removes it. So, too, Eisav becomes sullied with sin throughout the year and has no means of cleansing himself; but Yaakov becomes sullied with sin during the year, and when Yom Kippur comes he has a means of cleansing himself, as it says, *For on this day He will cleanse you...*

(*Bereishis Rabbah* 65:15)

Here the Midrash compares the cleansing process of Yom Kippur to the removal of grain husks. At this time of year, the crops are prepared to be gathered in and brought to the storehouses. Before this is done, and in order to render them fit for tithing, the husks, straw, and so on — the waste matter — are removed. Similarly, we remove our "waste matter" at this time — all the sins we have accumulated over the last year. Then our pure essence is ready to be brought to Hashem during Sukkos, the festival of ingathering.[3]

> ...and the festival of ingathering, at the end of the year, when you gather in your work from the field.
>
> (Shemos 23:16)

Ingathering and Unity

> You shall make a festival of Sukkos for yourselves, seven days, when you gather in from your barns and from your presses.
>
> (Devarim 16:13)

Sukkos is called the "festival of ingathering." At a physical level, this refers to collecting the crops. Having finished the process of harvesting and threshing, we are ready to bring the grain into the house. The results of the year's activities are collected together and brought into the house to sustain the family through the winter.

In the spiritual realm, there is also a process of ingathering at this time. The Jewish people assemble to unite with Hashem. Provided this is their goal, even the most disparate elements of the nation are brought together. This is represented by the four species of Sukkos. The *esrog* possesses a sweet taste and a beautiful aroma and is therefore representative of those who possess Torah learning and good deeds. The date palm, from which the *lulav* is taken, has fruit which possess taste but no aroma and symbolizes those who have only Torah learning but do not excel in good deeds. The *hadasim* possess a beautiful aroma but no taste and therefore represent those who have good deeds but no Torah learning. Finally, the *aravos* have neither taste nor aroma, and therefore represent those who have neither Torah learning nor good deeds. Let them unite together, says Hashem, and they will atone for each other.[4]

Full Circle

With the dropping of the seeds into the ground, the agricultural cycle has come full circle. Last year's seeds germinated, grew into plants, and are now giving their seeds back to the earth to begin the cycle again.

At the festival of Sukkos, we too come full circle. It is the final stage of the three festivals, following Pesach and Shavuos. These three festivals are not independent celebrations; they form a process, of which Sukkos is the culmination. Pesach launches the growth of the nation, Shavuos sees the peak of the nation's growth in terms of our acceptance of Torah, and Sukkos returns us to Hashem in a session of intense closeness.[5]

In both spiritual and physical spheres, then, we have come full circle. This explains the recurring motif of circles at this time. In the name and description of Sukkos, we repeatedly find the concept of circles, for example: "You shall celebrate [*tachogu*, literally, "encircle"] the festival [*chag*] of Hashem."[6] *Chag*, usually translated as "festival," is based on the root *chug*, "circle." Allegorically, then, this verse tells us to circle the circuits of Hashem, as described in an earlier verse:

...וחג האסיף תקופת השנה

The festival of ingathering, when the year comes full circle...[7]
(Shemos 34:22)

The motif of circles is found in the service of Sukkos, too. We circle the *sifrei Torah* with our *lulav* and *esrog* daily during Sukkos and perform this procedure seven times on Hoshana Rabbah. On Shemini Atzeres (Simchas Torah, for those outside Eretz Yisrael) we circle the *bimah* with *sifrei Torah* seven times. These *hakafos* (circuits) reflect the nature of Sukkos and fall seedtime.

Dust to Dust

Coming full circle in the agricultural cycle means that this year's crop has reached the end of its life. The plants lie withered and yellow with age. Their existence served only to feed man and to ensure a continuation of the crop's existence, through their seeds. Their brief span of life in the world is now over, having fulfilled their function.

The sukkah itself is a temporary dwelling and is a metaphor for existence in this world.

This provides an essential message for us. It is all too easy for us to see this world as all there is, as all that matters in life. But our task is to realize that this world is transitory, through which we are merely passing on our way to eternity. All we have in this world must be seen as nothing more than tools, with which to further our work of creating our portion in the World to Come.

Koheles presents this message most powerfully.

" 'Futility of futility,' says Koheles, 'futility of futilities; all is futility.' " Koheles speaks about the temporary nature of man's existence. It was the final work written by Shlomo HaMelech in his old age[8] and presents the view that nothing in this world is of lasting value. Everything must be seen for what it is — a temporary tool for reaching an eternal goal.

Everything comes from dust, and everything returns to dust.
(Koheles 3:20)

This is the story of the crops; this is the story of man. By appreciating the short-lived nature of this world, we are better able to use it properly in furthering our relationship with Hashem. And it is at this time of year that this relationship reaches fulfillment.

The Desire for Water

The four species are brought to influence a desire for water [rain]; just as these four species cannot survive without water, so too, the world cannot survive without water.
(*Ta'anis* 2b)

"On Chag [Sukkos], the world is judged with regard to its water" (Rosh HaShanah 16a).

The rainy season now approaches. The hot and dry summer is about to end, and the rains will soon penetrate the tilled earth. The need for these life-giving rains dominates the procedures of this time. When the Beis HaMikdash stood, the *nisuch hamayim*, "water-libation ceremony," took place during each day of Chol HaMo'ed. A golden jug was filled with three measures of water from the Shilo'ach, a well near Jerusalem. The shofar was sounded, and the *Kohen* ascended the *mizbei'ach* and poured the water into two silver basins. This procedure demonstrated that we were seeking rain from Hashem:[9]

Hashem says, "Pour water before Me on Sukkos, so that the rains of the year should be blessed for you."

(*Rosh HaShanah* 16a)

"Whoever did not see the simchah of the water-drawing ceremony never saw simchah in his lifetime!" (Sukkah 5:1).

The Marriage Canopy

Since the rain is the husband of the land, and the physical manifestation of Hashem's relationship with us, now is the time to fulfill this relationship. Sukkos is the time of the marriage between Hashem and the Jewish people.

When we examine the nature of Sukkos, the concept of marriage is clearly seen. First, the sukkah itself is symbolic of a *chuppah*, the canopy under which a marriage is performed.[10] The encircling of the *sifrei Torah* that takes place during Sukkos is analogous to the bride's encircling of the groom. Sukkos lasts for seven days (in Eretz Yisrael), the same length of time as wedding celebrations. There is great stress on *simchah*, "joy," during Sukkos; it is mentioned with regard to Sukkos on three occasions in the Torah,[11] and in the prayers we refer to Sukkos as "the time of our joy." This *simchah* is the same *simchah* as that of a marriage — the deep, inner joy that results from fulfillment. It is the completion attained with a needed and meaningful relationship that provides *simchah*.[12]

> So that your descendants should know [yeidu] that I housed the children of Yisrael in sukkos...
>
> (Vayikra 23:43)

This verse tells us that Sukkos provides *da'as*, "knowledge," of Hashem. *Da'as* always refers to being

able to connect to something. Thus it is used to describe relationships between man and wife: "And the
man *knew* Chavah, his wife; and she conceived and gave
birth to Kayin..."[13] Here we are told that Sukkos is an
opportunity to connect to Hashem.

One cannot love Hashem except through *da'as*, through
knowing Him...

(Rambam, *Hilchos Teshuvah* 10:6)

The Beginnings of Consummation

The eighth day...is an atzeres...

(Vayikra 23:36)

An atzeres — I have held you back *[atzarti]* with Me. It is
like a king who invites his sons to a feast for several days.
When the time arrives for them to leave he says, "My
sons! I beg of you, stay for one more day; it is difficult to
have you part from me."

(*Rashi* loc. cit.)

The essence of Shemini Atzeres, the festival immediately following Sukkos, is the intense closeness
between Hashem and the children of Yisrael at this
time. It is similar to the stage of *yichud*, "private meeting," between a groom and bride immediately following the *chuppah*.[14] It represents the beginnings of the
consummation of our relationship, as manifest by the
rains. It is from this day that the rains are expected.
The importance of rain to this time of year is highlighted by the prayer for rain we say on Shemini
Atzeres, as well as the addition to the Amidah that we
insert at this time — "He makes the wind blow and the
rain fall."

As Tishrei draws to a close and we enter Cheshvan, the rains begin to fall. The skies unite with the

earth, and Hashem unites with us in the consummation of our very special relationship.

> From when do we pronounce the blessing on rain? From
> when the groom [the rain] goes out to meet the bride
> [the earth].[15]
>
> What does one bless? Said Rabbi Yehudah in the name
> of Rav: "We thank You, Hashem our God, for every drop
> You bring down for us..."
>
> (*Ta'anis* 6b)

CHESHVAN

Seeds of Faithfulness

Rabbi Ami said: "The rain falls only through the merit of
the faithful..."

(*Ta'anis* 8a)

The sowing of seeds is a powerful demonstration
of *emunah*, "faithfulness." It is an act that, on the surface, is surprising. Rather than take all of the grain to
eat, man selects some of this perfectly good potential
food and buries it in the ground. He trusts in Hashem
to provide rain and to make the seeds grow into a new
crop.[1] For the atheist, sowing seeds is an act of faith in
nature; the Jew, however, has *emunah* that it is Hashem
causing the seeds to grow.[2] During the winter months,
as man prays for beneficial rains to make his crops
grow, he draws upon, and strengthens, his *emunah*.

*"And he shall be the
faithfulness of your times,
a store of salvation, wisdom, and knowledge..."
(Yeshayahu 33:6).
" 'The faithfulness' —
this refers to the Tal-
mudic order of Zera'im
[seeds]" (Shabbos 31a).*

> *To relate of Your kindness by morning and Your faithfulness by
> nights.*
>
> (Tehillim 92:3)

With the day being a microcosm of the year, winter has its equivalent in night. The night, too, is a time
for *emunah*. As we go to sleep, we entrust our souls to
Hashem, trusting that He will also be faithful and re-

"Anyone who does not re-
cite 'True and faithful is
all this...' in the evening
prayer has not fulfilled
his obligation" (Berachos
12a).

turn them to us in the morning. When we wake up, born anew, the first words we utter are "I thank you, O living and enduring King, that You have returned my soul to me in mercy — great is Your faithfulness!"

Hashem's kindness has not ceased; His mercy has not finished. They are new every morning — great is Your faithfulness!
(Eichah 3:22–23)

Rabbi Alexandri said: "Since You renew us every morning, we know Your faithfulness is great for the resurrection of the dead."
(*Eichah Rabbah* 3:8)

"Hashem exiled Yisrael
among the nations only
in order to increase the
number of converts, as it
says, 'And I will sow her
to me in the earth'
(Hoshea 2:25); a man
sows a se'ah of seed only
in order to bring in many
korin of produce"
(Pesachim 57b).

The winter is a time for *emunah* in another sense, too. The dark months of winter, themselves a macrocosm of night, are a microcosm of exile. *Emunah* is the trait with which we survive the oppression of exile. With enduring faithfulness to the truth of our covenant with Hashem at Sinai, we remain strong until the redemption comes.[3] The final redemption will bring with it *techiyas hameisim*, "the resurrection of the dead" — the ultimate kindness from Hashem. Our *emunah* in the rains of winter is also the *emunah* in *techiyas hameisim*. That is why both concepts are combined in the second *berachah* of the Amidah:[4] "He makes the wind blow and the rain fall...and You are faithful to resurrect the dead."

The Power of Life

"The day of the rainfall
is as great as the day of
the resurrection of the
dead" (Ta'anis 7a).

The role for *emunah* is not the only feature shared by rain and *techiyas hameisim*. They are conceptually similar in many ways. We already learned in "Nissan" about some of these. The decomposition and disintegration of the seed, which serves as a prelude to rebirth, is a precise parallel of *techiyas hameisim*. In both cases, the process which appears to be death is transformed into life.

Another common element is that both illustrate the *gevurah*, "might," of Hashem. The resurrection of the dead will clearly be one of the greatest miracles in history, going against all the "laws" of nature. It is something science cannot predict. In the same way, explains the Vilna Gaon,[5] rain is the one aspect of nature that is entirely unpredictable. The sun rises and sets predictably, the tides follow a set pattern, but the weather is beyond our comprehension.

"You are eternally mighty, Hashem; the Resuscitator of the dead are You, abundantly able to save, making the wind blow and the rain descend" (Shemoneh Esreh).

The Vilna Gaon wrote this in the eighteenth century. Earlier in our century, a challenge arose to this teaching. As computers became more advanced, they were employed for use with weather prediction. The great mathematician John Von Neumann predicted that it would soon be possible to construct a computer which could accurately forecast the weather. Most people accepted this. It seemed a reasonable idea; surely it was just a matter of programming in all the variables and their initial values. The rest would just be computation. Of course, there would be slight inaccuracies in recording the weather for the first setting, but these would be relatively insignificant.

They were proved spectacularly wrong. It was found that tiny variations in the initial settings would escalate to vast differences in just a few days. This is popularly known as "the butterfly effect," whereby the flapping of a butterfly's wings in China can have an escalating effect, which results in a tornado in America. It was realized that it would be impossible, even at a theoretical level, to forecast the weather beyond a few days. The pattern of the rains was universally acknowledged to be forever beyond our understanding.

First Rains

Cheshvan is the month in which we begin to request that the rains be unleashed from the heavens. We pray, "Give dew and rain *as a blessing*" — we want the rain to be of Divine essence, a gift from Above, rather than merely a natural process. These first rains are called *yoreh*, meaning "to teach," as in the word *torah*, "teachings." The Gemara states that the first rains teach people to waterproof their roofs, bring their produce into the house, and take care of their winter needs.[6] The rain is of essential importance, ensuring a food supply for the entire year.

"I shall give the rains of your land in its proper time, the early rains and the late rains..."
(Shema).

Although the Torah does not usually designate names for the months, preferring just to number them, Cheshvan is one of the few exceptions. In the verse describing the completion of the Beis HaMikdash, Cheshvan receives a name:

> *And in the eleventh year, in the month Bul, which is the eighth month, the house was finished...*
>
> (Melachim I 6:38)

Cheshvan is sometimes called "Marcheshvan"; one explanation is that mar means "drops," referring to the rainfall that begins in this month (Pri Chadash).

The word *bul* means "consume." With the addition of the letter *mem*, it becomes *mabul*, the great flood in the time of Noach which consumed the world[7] (*mem* has the numerical value forty, the number of days for which the rains fell). In this month, the rains of the Flood began to fall, and they eventually devastated the entire world.

We are therefore faced with a curious paradox. On the one hand, rain is a blessing, granting life to the world. On the other hand, rain was the tool Hashem used to annihilate the world. We need to further explore the nature of the winter rains.

Water and Torah

> The day of the rainfall is as great as the day on which the Torah was given...
>
> (*Ta'anis* 7a)

We noted that the name for the first rains, *yoreh*, is linguistically similar to *torah*. This indicates the wealth of parallels that exist between Torah and water. Here, in brief, are some:

- Just as water is delivered free to the world, so too is Torah free.[8]

- Just as water descends amid thunder and lightning, so too was the Torah delivered on Har Sinai amid thunder and lightning.[9]

- Just as water descends as tiny drops, yet gathers to form gigantic rivers, so too does one learn Torah little by little and eventually become a fountain of knowledge.[10]

- Just as water flows from a high place to a low place, so too does Torah knowledge flow away from those who are arrogant and toward those who are humble.[11]

- No one, when suffering from thirst, is ashamed to ask a lesser person for water. So, too, one who is thirsty for Torah is not ashamed to ask a person of lesser stature to teach him something.[12]

- Just as water descends from the Heavens, so too does Torah descend from the Heavens.[13]

" 'My gift shall pelt as the rain; my speech shall distill as the dew, as the small rain upon the grass, and as the showers upon the herbage' (Devarim 32:2). Gift means nothing other than Torah, as it says (Mishlei 4:2), 'For I have given you a good gift; do not forsake My Torah' " (Ta'anis 7a).

- Just as water brings life to the world, so too does Torah bring life to those who study it.[14]

Let us take a closer look at why water and Torah share the same features.

Form and Substance

Everything in the universe is made up of two elements: *tzurah*, "form," and *chomer*, "substance." Nothing can exist without having some dimension of *tzurah*; even the most shapeless jellyfish has a certain degree of form. And *tzurah* is nothing unless it has matter which it can combine with, some type of *chomer*.

In the world around us we see varying degrees of *tzurah*. At the lowest end of the scale is the desert — a shapeless mass of drifting sand dunes as far as the eye can see. At the highest end of the scale, in the wild, are the rainforests, complicated and intricate ecosystems teeming with life of all sorts.

What causes the difference between these two environments? Water. It is water that provides the fuel for the enormously complicated process known as life. It is water that descends from the heavens and bestows *tzurah* upon the world.

In man's environment we also find differing levels of *tzurah*. Some societies are a chaotic mess of crime and violence, achieving nothing at all. At the other end of the spectrum is the ideal Jewish city, with everyone working together to build a stable society in which man can fulfill his potential.

The difference between these two extremes is Torah. To the extent that there is an order of morality in the world, it is due to the penetration of the Torah into the Jewish people and beyond. As the Torah descends from the Heavens, *tzurah* is bestowed upon a world of *chomer*.

The power of *tzurah* that comes down from the heavens therefore has two manifestations. It has a spiritual manifestation of Torah, a code of morality and order. And it has a physical manifestation of water, the fuel for life's development.

Waters of Life and Death

At the time of Noach, there was an increased influx of *tzurah* from above. Hashem wanted to give the Torah to that generation. But they were not ready to receive it. Steeped in sin, they were not worthy to receive the *tzurah* of the Torah. Their society, in which licentiousness and robbery were rampant, was the antithesis of the *tzurah* of Torah.

But when Hashem sends down *tzurah*, it *will* impose itself. And if the people are not ready to receive it, it will impose itself insofar as to wipe out the anti-*tzurah* that is being displayed by the people.

Thus, the generation of Noach was annihilated. The rains that fell had the capacity to grant life. But since the people were not ready to receive true life, it wiped them out in preparation for a generation that would be ready. The forty days of rain set the stage for Moshe's forty-day stay on Har Sinai, in which he brought down the Torah for the Jewish people.

It was specifically an overabundance of rain that destroyed the world. This was measure-for-measure retribution for that generation's sin. They believed in breaking all boundaries, in having no limitations.[15] All moral laws were broken, and because of their sin of theft their fate was sealed, for theft demonstrated their total lack of regard for interpersonal boundaries. Thus, Hashem too, did not limit Himself. He gave rain. And more rain. And more rain. Until they were entirely wiped out. Hashem echoed their policy of breaking all limits.

Kiss of Life

Cheshvan is the month in which the life-giving winter rains begin to fall. It is the month in which Heaven and Earth meet, in a marriage of *tzurah* with *chomer*. But there is also a position in space through which this interface is channeled. That is the Beis HaMikdash, the place "where Heaven and Earth kiss."[16] Thus, we find that the Beis HaMikdash was completed in the month of Cheshvan. The Midrash also states that every year after the Flood there was an enormously heavy rainfall for forty days each year, an aftereffect of the Flood, beginning on the first of Cheshvan. This ceased with the completion of the Beis HaMikdash.[17] The Beis HaMikdash provided a chance to correct the crime of that generation, a new opportunity for *tzurah* to unite with *chomer*.

"From the day the Beis HaMikdash was destroyed, the rains dried up for the world; in some years there is plenty of rain, but in some years there is only a little rain..." (Ta'anis 19b).

The constellation of this month is עקרב (*akrav*), the scorpion. The name for this deadly creature is composed of the words עוקר בית (*oker bayis*), "destruction of the House." But it can also be read as עיקר בית (*ikar bayis*), "foundation of the House," Cheshvan being the month in which the third Beis HaMikdash will be initiated.[18] This dual meaning of *akrav* signifies the duality of Cheshvan. In this month, the floodgates of Torah knowledge are opened. Paralleling this, the rainfall begins. This can grant *tzurah* to the world or damage it. It all depends on how open and willing we are to receive instruction and order. The choice is ours.

חרף

DEEP WINTER

KISLEV

The Winter Nights

We now enter the season of *choref*, "deep winter." A new era has clearly arrived in nature. No more are the long and sunny summer days. Now we have rain and snow and long, dark nights. It is the "night" section of the year, when the moon is dominant rather than the sun.

In terms of the spiritual calendar, a new era is also clearly beginning. The sequence of Biblically ordained festivals has finished. In the winter months, the only festivals are the rabbinically ordained Chanukah and Purim.[1] This change parallels the change in nature noted above. The relationship of the Oral Torah, in which these festivals are prescribed, to the Written Torah, is identical to that of the moon to the sun. Just as the moon produces no light of its own, but reflects that of the sun, so too does the Oral Torah build itself up from analyzing and developing the Written Torah. It "reflects" the rich databank of the Written Torah.[2] This pattern is discerned in the two festivals that are linked to Torah. Shavuos, the giving of the Written Torah, is in summer, while Chanukah, which represents the triumph of the Oral Torah, is in winter.

"Choref is so named because we now plant those crops which are quick [charifin] in ripening" (Rashi on Bereishis 8:22).

" '[Moshe] was there [on Har Sinai] with Hashem for forty days and nights' (Shemos 34:28). How did Moshe know when it was day and when it was night? When Hashem taught him the Written Torah, he knew it was day, and when He taught him the Oral Torah, he knew it was night" (Midrash Tanchuma, Ki Sissa 36).

Seasonal Festivities

Kislev is best known as the month in which Chanukah occurs. In fact, it has a much older significance for festivals, dating back to the beginning of history itself:

> The [non-Jewish festival] Calenda is during the eight days following the [winter] solstice.
>
> Adam HaRishon saw [as winter progressed] the days becoming increasingly shorter in length. "Woe to me," he said. "Perhaps it is because of my sin that the world is becoming dark, and it will return to its state of turmoil and nothingness, and this is the death that has been imposed upon me by Heaven!" He went and fasted and prayed for eight days. But when *tekufas Teves* [the winter solstice] arrived, and he saw the days progressively increasing in length, he said, "It is just the way of the world!" He went and celebrated for eight days. The next year, he designated both sets [of eight days] as festivals. He did this for the sake of Heaven, while they [the non-Jews] designated them for idolatry.[3]
>
> (*Avodah Zarah* 8a)

In this fascinating paragraph, we learn of an ancient festival that is unheard of now, and yet strikes a note of *déjà vu* within us. Two notes, in fact. On the one hand, an eight-day festival concerning light in winter seems remarkably similar to Chanukah, the eight-day festival of lights. On the other hand, *l'havdil*, we know that Christianity, which has its roots in idolatry, celebrates its main festival at that time of year, which also has an eight-day structure (they celebrate his circumcision, eight days after his birth). And although that festival itself is not called "Calenda," the Christians did name their system of time measurement "calendar." Let us further explore the season of the solstice.

Primal Darkness

In the beginning, God created the heavens and the earth. The earth was void and empty, and there was darkness on the face of the deep.

(Bereishis 1:1–2)

Darkness — this refers to the exile of Yavan [Greece]...
(*Bereishis Rabbah* 2:4)

When the world was created, there were certain imperfections built into it. These are the states of void, emptiness, darkness, and deep of which the Torah speaks. These primal imperfections have been manifest during history as four evil empires that have risen against the Jewish people.[4] Darkness, we are told, represents Yavan.

This may strike us as peculiar. Of all the descriptions that could be used for Yavan, darkness seems to be the least appropriate. Evil, yes. Destructive, undoubtedly. But darkness? Greece was a source of enlightenment for mankind; they brought the light of understanding into a world of confusion. The natural sciences all have their roots in ancient Greece. We certainly do not see anything inherently evil in science — it is knowledge, albeit of a secular nature. How can we use the term *darkness* to describe such a nation?

Concealment

The darkness of which we are speaking means much more than just an absence of light. It refers to concealment, a mask that serves to obscure something. That something is Hashem, and the mask is nature.

Hashem does not reveal His presence openly. Were He to do so, there would be no room for free will.

There could be no reward for performing Hashem's will if His presence were obvious. Therefore, Hashem created a mask to disguise His omnipotence. Nature serves to present a natural system of how the world is run, which could be taken at face value alone. One can look at the world and be fooled by the mask, or one can look beyond the mask and see Hashem behind everything. One can focus on the concealment, on the darkness, or on the light beneath.

The world is called "olam," which is based on the word ha'alamah, "concealment."

Yavan saw the darkness. The wisdom the Greeks considered so important is indeed important, but only when viewed from the correct perspective. Scientific descriptions of the world must not be seen as the absolute portrayal of reality. They have to be understood as explaining only the disguise Hashem uses. Yavan, however, said that "what you see is what you get." This superficial understanding of the universe Yavan presented was the ultimate concealment, the ultimate darkness.

"Woe to them...who put darkness for light and light for darkness!" (Yeshayahu 5:20).

> *Darkness* — this refers to the exile of Yavan, who darkened the perspective of Yisrael with their decrees, telling them, "Write on the horn of an ox that you have no share in the God of Yisrael!"
>
> (*Bereishis Rabbah* 2:4)

The threat of Yavan was their imposition of their darkness upon us. It was not that they denied the existence of Hashem; rather, they denied that He has anything to do with the day-to-day running of the world. They told the Jews to write that "you have no share in the God of Yisrael" — not that there is no God, but that He has nothing to do with us.[5] Hellenism was a lifestyle that viewed only the superficialities of existence without attributing any hidden depths to it.

The Jewish people see beyond this concealment. We have the Torah of light, which keeps us in touch with Hashem. The Torah serves as a guide to show exactly how Hashem controls everything that exists. The light of Hashem's presence is the light that conquered the primal darkness:

The Hebrew word for the natural world, hateva (הטבע), is of the same numerical value as Elokim (אלוקים), "God."

> And God said, "Let there be light." And there was light.
>
> (Bereishis 1:3)

With this understanding of the difference between Yavan and Yisrael, we can understand what lay behind the battles that took place. We may wonder what the Hasmoneans were thinking, to engage in a war in which they were hopelessly outnumbered. How could such a ragtag group hope to fight the vast Greek army with its war elephants? Yet now we can understand what gave them the courage, and the victory. For they had already won the real battle, the battle of ideologies, of recognizing the hand of Hashem behind the darkness of nature. So what difference do numbers make? Hashem controls everything — it is He Who determines the victor. Those who stand for light are destined to overcome those who stand for darkness. And the Jews were indeed victorious.

The name Mattisyahu means "gift of God," demonstrating his awareness that everything is in Hashem's hands. Similarly, Yochanan means "Hashem bestows" (Pri Tzaddik, Chanukah 14).

Emerging Glory

This outlook of the Hasmoneans was their successful response to the glory of Greece. The hallmark of Greece was beauty, but there was no glory in that beauty.

Glory is called *hod* in the Torah, which is related to the word *hoda'ah*, meaning to "acknowledge" or "to give way." *Hod* occurs, for example, when the external, limiting nature of something gives way before its inner essence.[6] *Hod* occurs when a handicapped person manages to coordinate a sequence of movements out of sheer willpower, not letting himself be hindered by physical limitations. His inner drive bursts forth, and his body gives way to it. That is true *hod*.

Yavan may make a superficial attempt to recognize this with the Special Olympics, but their real champions, the ones who receive the fame and fortune, are always the winners of the "real" Olympic games. Ultimately, Yavan cares only for those who possess external beauty and perfection, caring little for inner energy. That is why they are able to match people against each other in competition — for the externalities of people can be measured against each other and timed on the clock. We, on the other hand, would never pit people against each other. For the only true value of people is engendered by their inner essence, and the only One who can measure that is Hashem Himself.

The *hod* of the Hasmoneans was the result of their drive to stay true to Hashem, overcoming their natural limitations. They perceived that Hashem was behind everything, and they made everything within themselves give way to Him. As a result, their inner strengths poured forth beyond their wildest dreams. That was the *hod* of Chanukah, which we are enjoined to emulate.

The Light of the Olive

> *I shall be as the dew to Yisrael...and his hod shall be as that of the olive...*
>
> (Hoshea 14:6–7)

The victory of Chanukah was the victory of inner essence over external appearances, of light over darkness. The menorah is an apt banner of this victory. For the light of the menorah comes from the olive. The olive seems to be just a small fruit like any other, not at all special. But this is only on the outside. There is so much more to the olive than meets the eye. Inside this tiny fruit is oil that can light an entire room. The olive's *hod* is that its external appearance is surpassed by its inner light.[7]

The olive serves to remind us that if we look beyond the superficialities of this world, beyond the mask darkness, we can perceive light. The light of the olive is the light of the Torah's wisdom, the light which illuminates Hashem's control of the world.

Perhaps we can see this message in an even stronger way. The olives which are on the trees at the moment, late in the season, have been darkening from green to black. It is these black olives which contain the most oil. The blacker the olive, the more light it

" 'And Yo'av sent to Teko'ah and took from there a wise woman...' (Shmuel II 12:2). What was special about Teko'ah? Rabbi Yochanan said: 'Because they frequently consume olive oil, they possess wisdom' " (Menachos 85b).

contains. The more we recognize nature for what it is, as darkness, as concealment, the better we are able to perceive the light behind it.

The lighting of the menorah by the Hasmoneans was the victory of understanding that there is so much more to the world than meets the eye. And Hashem replied in kind: I'll show you that there's even more to the world than you think. You think that there's enough oil in this vial for only one night? I'll show you that there is enough light in this vial for eight nights!

"If one sees olive oil in a dream, he can look forward to the illumination of Torah" (Berachos 57a).

The light of the menorah is the light of Hashem's presence. The thirty-six flames that we light on Chanukah are sparks of the thirty-six hours of the Divine light that shone at the dawn of time, and that conquered the primal darkness, before being put away for the righteous to enjoy in the final redemption.[8]

The Olive Apart

The Greeks did not want to kill us. They wanted to assimilate us into their culture. We won by remaining separate, by retaining our identity as Jews:

"Olive trees cannot be successfully hybridized with other trees" (Yerushalmi, Kelayim 1:7). This teaches us that the Jewish people are destined to remain separate from the other nations (Meshech Chachmah, parashas Bechukosai).

A moist olive tree, fair with pleasant fruit, is what Hashem called your name...

(Yirmeyahu 11:16)

Other liquids mix together, but olive oil remains separate. So, too, is Yisrael separate from other nations...

(Shemos Rabbah 36)

Olive oil represents the singularity of our identity. Rather than succumb to Greek culture, we remained true to the Torah. The Written Torah was translated into Greek and stolen from us; but with the Oral Torah, we retained our uniqueness. The thirty-six lights of Chanukah also represent the thirty-six tractates of the Babylonian Talmud with which we resisted Hellenism.

Spark of the Solstice

Now we can well understand the connection with the festival of Adam HaRishon. For Chanukah celebrates the victory of light emerging from darkness. The winter solstice, when the light of the sun begins to grow again, is the essence of Chanukah. This light may appear to be only sunlight, but on this day it is a refraction of the primal light that shone at the dawn of time.[9]

At the microcosm of the day, the solstice is paralleled by "midnight, when an influence of illumination and favor emanates from Hashem to all worlds...and the spiritual illumination of the day begins to be awakened, until daybreak...when all existence is renewed" (Derech Hashem 4:6:1).

The Chanukah of the Hasmoneans had a chronological as well as conceptual link with the winter solstice. In that year, the longest night, the height of Yavan's darkness, fell on the twenty-fifth of Kislev.[10] It was on that day that the tide was turned conclusively in favor of the Jews and the Beis HaMikdash was rededicated. It was from then that the light began to grow.

The word *chanukah* is based on the root *chinnuch*, which means "initiation" or "beginning." On Chanukah, the spark of the Divine light begins to shine. The victory of Chanukah is the first flame of redemption, a light that reaches its full illumination with the coming of Mashiach.[11]

"The people who walk in darkness saw a great light..." (Yeshayahu 9:1).

And Hashem shall be for you as an eternal light...
(Yeshayahu 60:19)

The Brazen Leopard

Daniel spoke, and said, "I saw in my vision by night...four great beasts... The first was like a lion...and behold, another beast, a second one, similar to a bear... Afterwards I beheld, and there was another, similar to a leopard..."

(Daniel 7:2–6)

In Daniel's vision, where the four beasts represented the four exiles to which we have been subjected, the leopard was the parallel of Yavan. This is because

"Just as the leopard [namer], is variegated [menumar] in its coloration, so did Yavan impose 'variegated' decrees on Yisrael [i.e., decrees which differed widely from each other]" (Rashi on Daniel 7:6).

they both share the same trait — that of *azus*. *Azus* is based on the word *az*, "strength," but it relates to an inner rather than outer strength. It is often translated as "brazenness"[12] or "chutzpah," but it also carries the connotation of defiance, meaning "to oppose" or "contend" with something.

Leopards are not especially large predators. The Israeli subspecies weighs up to about eighty pounds, the African around two hundred. Yet they take on prey many times their own size, in fierce brazenness. In the words of the curator of the Hai-Bar nature reserve of the Negev, Bill Clark: "They don't have the speed of a cheetah, nor can they claim the brute force of a lion. Instead, they rely on their wits. They're smart, and, pound for pound, they're the scrappiest of the big cats... No other predator confronts its victims with such rampaging fury."

"The leopard is a hybrid of the lion and the wild boar" (Magen Avos on Avos 5:20). This means that Yavan combined the traits of Bavel and Edom (Reb Tzadok, Likutei Ma'amarim, s.v. "u'lekach parashiyos"). It also denotes its azus, the trademark of illegitimate birth (Maseches Kallah 2).

This brazen defiance, coupled with intelligence, was the hallmark of Yavan. Most nations would be content to just have their own ideology. But not Yavan. Yavan was violently antagonistic to any outlook that differed from theirs. Totally opposed to any kind of tolerance, they fought anything and everything.[13] They defiled the Beis HaMikdash, and they forced Yisrael to discard a Torah lifestyle:

> I saw in my vision...another, like a leopard — this refers to Yavan, which set up decrees and told Yisrael: "Write on the horn of an ox that you have no share in the World to Come!"
>
> (*Vayikra Rabbah* 13:5)

The Leopard Victorious

The brazen person is destined for Gehinnom.

(*Avos* 5:25)

Of all the big cats, it is only the leopard, and its South American equivalent, the jaguar, which often appear in black forms. Perhaps this expresses Yavan's nature of darkness.

Azus is not merely a harmful trait — it is one of the very worst characteristics. It stands at odds with the Jew's sense of shame, which keeps him from sin. Yet no character trait is *entirely* good or bad. All traits can be used either way, and *azus* is no exception:

> Be...brazen as a leopard...to fulfill the will of your Father in Heaven.

> (Ibid., 24)

The Greeks used *azus* in a negative way. But the Hasmoneans were victorious over the Greeks. Victory does not just mean military or even ideological conquest. It means that one takes the enemy's evil trait and uses it for the good.[14] Then one has truly conquered the enemy, which is really the enemy within.

One perspective of the leopard's brazenness is that it stands unafraid of creatures that outweigh it or outnumber it. It does not feel confined by its natural limitations. Such was the quality of the Hasmoneans. They were far outnumbered by the gigantic Greek army. But they stood firm by their beliefs, never being scared away. Knowing they were fighting for Hashem and His Torah, they were not discouraged by their "natural" limitations.[15]

"Yisrael are the most brazen of nations" (Beitzah 25b).

The Leopard's Learning

A bashful person cannot learn...

(Ibid. 2:5)

Azus is also integral to the Oral Torah with which we conquered Greek philosophy. Although a sense of shame is usually a virtue, and one of the hallmarks of the Jewish people, it is not desirable in the study of Oral Torah.[16] When learning Torah, one must seek the truth. A person must always ask questions when he does not understand something. If he fails to ask out of fear of appearing foolish, he will never learn. When two people are arguing over the correct explanation in a section of Gemara, each must be concerned only with reaching the true explanation. A person must never cower into submission to accept an explanation he has reason to feel is incorrect. (Clearly, if the presenter of the explanation is of a greater level of scholarship, one must try harder to understand rather than dismiss his explanation.)

The *Tur*,[17] discussing the maxim that one should

be brazen as a leopard, presents King David as the quintessential example of the type of *azus* that is required, citing the following verse:

And I shall speak your statutes in front of kings [referring to Torah scholars[18]] and not be ashamed.

(Tehillim 119:46)

King David spoke that which he felt to be the truth and was not ashamed to do so. This is one of the reasons why he is described as being the quintessence of the Oral Torah.[19] This quality of *azus*, which he practiced to perfection, was his heritage from his ancestor Bo'az. Bo'az wished to marry Rus, but was challenged by the law that one may not marry a Moabite. He "sped like a leopard," says the *Yerushalmi*,[20] and expounded that one must take into account the precision of the wording; the law was specifically speaking about a Moabite, not a Moabitess. He had the *azus* of the leopard within him (hence the name *Bo'az*, "in him is brazenness"), which enabled his descendant David to triumph in Torah against all opposition.

Rus also possessed the trait of azus; the nation of Mo'av originates in the incestuous relationship of Lot with his daughter, and we are told that descendants of illegitimate births possess azus.

Alert as an Almond

נמר שקד על עריהם...

The leopard is poised alert [shokeid] over the city...

(Yirmeyahu 5:6)

This verse associates the leopard with the quality of *shekeidah*. *Shekeidah* refers to continual eagerness, alertness, vigilance. It is all very well to possess the quality of *azus*, but one might not make use of this trait without the zealousness of *shekeidah*. It is not enough to just be able to stand up against the threat of an alien nation — one has to actually do so. The Hasmoneans

It is interesting to note that Aharon's staff produced shekeidim (see Bemidbar 17:24); Aharon is the symbol of the Oral Torah (and also of hod).

utilized the characteristic of *azus* only with the benefit of their *shekeidah*. The combination of these two properties enabled them to defeat Yavan.

Almonds are called *shekeidim*. This is because the almond tree is the very first tree to blossom, as soon as the rains ease off. Thus the almond represents assiduousness and zeal. That is why we find that *shekeidim* are integral to the Menorah, the symbol of the Chanukah victory:[21]

And you shall make a Menorah...three cups made like almonds on each branch...four bowls like almonds on the candlestick...

(Shemos 25:31, 33)

An attitude of *shekeidah* toward Torah is therefore a prerequisite for dealing with Yavan:[22]

Be vigilant [*shokeid*] in learning Torah and know what to answer a heretic...

(*Avos* 2:14)

This is undoubtedly stated with regard to Greek philosophy...

(Maharal, *Nesivos Olam* 1, p. 62)

"Hashem said to Yisrael:... 'I am giving you the Torah so that you should busy yourselves with it constantly: "Happy is the man who listens to me, to be diligent [lishkod] at my door!" ' (Mishlei 8:34)" (Shemos Rabbah 25).

It is with zeal and vigilance that we must approach the Torah if it is going to help us tackle the ideology of Yavan. The threat of assimilation is one that gnaws away at the foundations of our beliefs. It is only with constant vigilance and dedication to Torah values that one can withstand it. This *shekeidah* is the key to our victory.

The Hare Queen

Of the four non-kosher animals listed in the Torah, the hare parallels Yavan. The reasons given for this are as follows:[23]

- Just as the hare is *ma'aleih geirah*, "raises up its cud," so did Yavan raise up its voice in praise of Hashem. When Alexander of Macedon saw Shimon HaTzaddik, he proclaimed, "Blessed is Hashem, the God of Shimon HaTzaddik!"

- Just as the hare brings up its cud, so did Yavan "bring up" (i.e., support) *tzaddikim*. Alexander respected Shimon HaTzaddik because he saw him in a dream before each of his successful battles.

- The hare is *ma'aleih geirah*, "brings up its cud." So too

Yavan dragged along (*megarer*, based on the word *geirah*) another kingdom after it — Edom.

- Ptolemy's mother was called "Hare" (in its Greek equivalent). When the Sages were forced to translate the Torah into Greek, they dared not translate *arneves* as "hare," in case the Greeks thought they were insulting her. So they translated it as "little legs," in reference to the hare's front legs being disproportionately smaller than its hind legs.

Dormant Slumber

The difference between our worldview and that of the Greeks is brought out in other ways during Kislev. The *Sefer Yetzirah* connects each month with a different action. Kislev, it states, is associated with *sheinah*, "sleep."

In the thick of the winter, the night section of the year, nature sleeps. Many of the animals are in hibernation, the several-month-long state of suspended animation. Much of the plant kingdom, too, lies dormant. The concept of sleep, however, is broader than just the state of physical slumber. It relates to dormancy and inactivity, when nothing changes. Metaphorically, this relates to the functioning of the world according to Yavan's perspective. When the world "sleeps," it is operating in a mode similar to that of autopilot on an airplane. It means that Hashem moves aside, so to speak, and runs the world according to the rules of nature without interfering to make any changes.[24]

ואין כל חדש תחת השמש.

There is nothing new under the sun.

(Koheles 1:9)

Koheles is not musing philosophically; he is describing the universe. "Under the sun" relates to that which is under the order of nature, the sun being the dominant body under which material development takes place. The sun itself always looks the same size, never changing. Under this order, there is nothing new. Everything operates according to the laws of nature. There is no supernatural interference; nature simply runs its course.

The sun provides the basis for the year. The year is called *shanah*, which is related to the word *sheinah*, "sleep." The solar year is associated with the dormant operation of the world. *Shanah* is also related to *yashan*, "old." In this system, there is nothing new, nothing *chadash*. Everything runs deterministically.

Yavan subscribed wholeheartedly to this view. And they were right, for this is indeed the system that governs them (although we know that in fact nature is just a mask for Hashem's workings). But we, the Jewish people, are governed by a different order. We are not under the sun — we are under the moon, which is renewal incarnate. There is nothing deterministic about our lives. We experience supernatural control *all the time*[25] That is not an exaggeration; the very existence of the Jewish people is a miracle. We are under Hashem's close control, and we must remain loyal to this knowledge.

TEVES

Lunar Conquest

Rosh Chodesh Teves falls during Chanukah. That Chanukah contains a Rosh Chodesh within-it relates to the nature of Chanukah itself. We already learned about the threat of Yavan, the ideology that the world follows an unmanned, natural course of events, under the dormant regime of the unchanging sun. They presented a perspective which was entirely deterministic, a life under the sun where there is nothing new.

But within Chanukah itself there is Rosh Chodesh. Within Chanukah itself there is the awareness that we need not be under the sun, for we have the moon. Within Chanukah itself comes the message that there *is* renewal and change, that one can escape the unchanging determinism of nature and place oneself under Hashem's direct rule.[1]

Yavan imposed a ban on kiddush hachodesh, "sanctification of the moon," the threat to their ideology.

Roots of Destruction

The month of Teves is extremely harsh for the Jewish people. The fast day that was instituted on the tenth of the month commemorates the tragic events that took place on that day and the preceding two days:

- On the eighth of the month, Ptolemy, ruler of Greece, forced the Sages to translate the Torah into Greek (the Septuagint). As we learned in "Kislev," this was part of the threat to our identity that Yavan presented. We are told that when this took place, three days of darkness descended on the world.

- On the ninth of the month, Ezra and Nechemiah died. Also on this day, the leader of Christianity was born.[2]

- On the tenth of the month, Yerushalayim was attacked by Nevuchadnetzar, king of Bavel. He laid a siege on the city, which resulted in the walls being breached on the seventeenth of Tamuz, three years later.

Although the actual destruction of the Beis HaMikdash took place on the ninth of Av, the tenth of Teves is of significance in its being the time when the process of destruction began.[3]

Fire and Ice

The oppressive heat of summer demonstrated the *churban* of Tamuz and Av. Mirroring this, we have the harsh storms of winter in Teves, another month of destruction.[4]

In both cases, the weather also reflects the type of sins that bring on *churban*. The heat of Tamuz relates to negative prohibitions transgressed with the fires of desire. The cold of Teves signifies a different type of sin — the neglect of positive commandments caused by our cooling off toward Hashem. The assimilation that

Yavan and Edom threaten us with leads us to cool down toward the Torah. Our observance of mitzvos becomes lax, and we shrug off our conscience. The flame of our soul grows cold.[5]

The punishments for each sin differ, as appropriate. Gehinnom has a section of fire and a section of icy snow.[6] Each is designed for its own type of sin. Our task during Teves is to keep the fire in our souls burning, to approach our Judaism with zest and energy.

The Rise of Rome

Teves is the beginning of all destruction. This means that Edom (Rome; Western civilization) has its power rooted in this month. Furthermore, we see that many of our problems with Yavan took place in this month (such as the translation of the Torah). Greece is considered the origin of the Roman empire, for with Alexander's expanding Greek empire came the eventual spread and triumph of Rome.[7] The month of Teves is therefore associated with Eisav, otherwise known as Edom.

"In the beginning, God created the Heavens and the Earth. The Earth was void and empty, and there was darkness on the face of the deep" (Bereishis 1:1–2). "Darkness refers to Yavan; the deep refers to Edom" (Bereishis Rabbah 2:4). Yavan was "on the face of" Edom, the root and source of it.

In "Kislev," we learned about the relationship between Chanukah and the winter solstice. For the purposes of our festival, we consider the lunar date of that event as it occurred at the time of the Hasmoneans. However, according to the current calendar, the winter solstice usually occurs during Teves (and is called *tekufas Teves* in the Gemara). We learned that Adam instituted an eight-day festival following the solstice, a festival which the non-Jews later adapted to idolatry and called Calenda. The modern manifestation of this is clear: Rome took upon itself the religion of Christianity, which celebrates its main festival in this month (and also has an eight-day period). Additionally, *Calenz* is known as the first day of the Roman calendar (January 1). Thus the winter solstice can also contain within it the beginnings of Rome's power.[8]

If we think back to what we learned about the construction of the Jewish calendar (in part 1), this is clearly understandable. Yaakov counts according to the moon, and Eisav counts according to the sun. We learned that the sun represents material wealth and instant gratification. These are the desires of Eisav and Rome. That is why the Roman calendar begins (approximately) with the solstice, the strengthening of the sun. Additionally, their day begins at 12 A.M., the equivalent of the winter solstice in terms of the day.

The sun also represents the ideology of Edom as an outgrowth of Yavan. The sun signifies the precedence of the natural order of the world. In contrast, we base our calendar on the moon, whose ever-changing appearance denotes our position above the determinism of nature.

The Irate Goat

The zodiacal sign of Teves is *gedi*, the goat (Capricorn). The goat is given other names in the Torah, such as *se'ir* and *eiz*. Both of these names are highly significant for Teves, as it relates to Eisav and Rome.

> *Yaakov said to his mother, Rivkah, "But my brother, Eisav, is a hairy man [ish se'ir], and I am smooth-skinned. Suppose my father feels me — I will appear to him as an impostor!' "*
>
> (Bereishis 27:11–12)

Se'ir means "hairy" and refers to goats, which are extremely hairy. But we are also being told here that the goat itself is a metaphor for Eisav.[9] The goat is also a metaphor for Yavan, as it appeared in Daniel's vision:

And the rough goat is the king of Yavan.

(Daniel 8:21)

In which way does the goat represent Yavan and Rome? One aspect is in the name itself — *eiz* — which means *azus*. The goat is not known for its tractability. It possesses the brazenness that is the hallmark of Yavan and the legacy of Eisav and Rome.[10]

The goat is the brazen one of the domesticated animals.[11]

(*Beitzah* 25b)

Prior Darkness

There is another aspect of the goat which relates to Yavan and Rome:

Why do goats go out [to pasture] first, and only afterward sheep?... It is like the creation of the world: first was darkness, and then came light.

(*Shabbos* 77b)

Rashi explains that goats are usually black (and sheep, of course, are white). Thus the goats, which push ahead to be first, symbolize the primal darkness, and the sheep which follow are the light which follows the darkness.

Here we clearly see the themes we have previously discussed. The goat, which represents Yavan, also echoes the darkness, the concealment, which is so fundamental to Yavan's outlook. It is this reign of darkness that always comes first. At the time of the creation of the world, there was first darkness over the face of the deep, and only then did Hashem create light. At the time of the second Beis HaMikdash, the Grecian empire brought three days of darkness in Teves when they forced the Sages to translate the Torah. It was only many years afterward that the Hasmoneans managed to conquer this with the light of Torah. This is represented by the white sheep, which portray the Jewish people, whose shepherd is Hashem:

> *He made His own people go out like sheep and guided them in the wilderness like a flock.*
>
> (Tehillim 78:52)

Trembling Rage

The irate anger of the goat is termed *rogez*,[12] and the *Sefer Yetzirah* states that *rogez* is the dominant emotion of this month. *Rogez* refers to a trembling feeling. We find that one can tremble in rage or tremble in fear:[13]

> One should always make one's good inclination tremble [in fear] and thus defeat the evil inclination, as it states, *Tremble and do not sin!* (Tehillim 4:5).
>
> (Berachos 5a)

A genuine fear of Hashem is a good deal more than just intellectual awareness of His existence. It is a sharply sensitive consciousness that causes us to tremble at the thought of the presence of the Creator. With this emotion, we can firmly reject the enticements of the evil inclination. Any desires to sin against the Master of the universe will seem preposterous. *Rogez*, the motif of Teves, may have the negative manifestation of fiery anger, but it also has a positive application.[14]

Perhaps we can also see the concept of *rogez* in the

general temper of nature at this time. *Rogez* is a term frequently used to describe violent weather conditions:

> *The waters saw you, they were afraid; the depths also* trembled. *The clouds poured out water...the lightning lit the world, and the earth* trembled *and shook.*
>
> (Tehillim 77:17–19)

"O Hashem, amidst Your rogez, remember mercy!" (Chavakuk 3:2).

Teves, in the heart of winter, is susceptible to harsh storms. Although we have repeatedly discussed the importance of rain, it is possible to have too much of a good thing:

> Fortunate is the year in which Teves is a widow....
>
> (*Ta'anis* 6b)

Since the land is the wife of the rain, if the rains stop, the land is "widowed." This is desirable for two reasons:

> Some say, because the places of Torah dissemination will not be empty [as their access routes will be usable]. Others say, because it will prevent the crops from being subject to blight.
>
> Is this so? But didn't Rabbi Chisda state, "Fortunate is the year in which Teves is unseemly [muddy]"? This is not a problem; our statement is referring to where rain fell previously, and his statement is referring to where rain did not fall previously.
>
> (Ibid., translated according to *Rashi*)

Rain represents our relationship with Hashem and, as such, is a good thing. But, as we learned in "Cheshvan" in connection with the Flood, it can also be a tool of destruction. It all depends on us, on how deserving we are of having a proper relationship with Hashem.

The First Light of Redemption

Esther was taken to King Achashveirosh, to his royal house, in the tenth month, the month of Teves....

(Esther 2:16)

There is a seeming superfluity in this verse; once we have been told that it was the tenth month, why do we need to be told that it was Teves?

The answer is that the placement of Esther in the king's palace was the first stage for the eventual salvation of the Jews. Amid the darkness, the light began to shine. The verse is highlighting Teves as it is the power of that month which provides the first step to salvation.[15] The winter solstice, which usually occurs during Teves, and is therefore called *tekufas Teves*, is not only significant for Eisav. As we noted in "Kislev," the beginning of the increase in sunlight is the first light of redemption, a light that will continue to grow over Shevat and Adar and will reach its full strength in Nissan.

קר

LATE WINTER

SHEVAT

Overflowing Water

The final season of the Jewish year is late winter, called *"kor"* (cold). We finish the year with Shevat and Adar, the eleventh and twelfth months.

The constellation of Shevat is the *d'li*, "bucket" (Aquarius). The concept of the *d'li* is expressed in Bilam's blessing to the desert camp of the Jewish people:

> *Water will overflow from his bucket, and his crops will have abundant water.*
>
> (Bemidbar 24:7)

At this stage of the year, most of the rains have fallen.[1] The rivers and streams are flowing in full force, and the land is saturated with rain. Drawing water does not require one to lower the bucket deep into the well; merely dipping it in at the top will bring it up overflowing with water.

The effects of the abundance of water are felt throughout the natural world. The trees now begin a new cycle of growth, a fresh burst of life which is sustained by the year's rains:

The first day of Shevat is the New Year for trees, according to Beis Shammai; Beis Hillel state that it is on the fifteenth of the month.

(Rosh HaShanah 2a)

Shevat is the month of the New Year for trees. The sap begins to rise through the trunks and branches[2] as the trees prepare to show the effects of the waters of winter. It is from this year's rains that all subsequent growth is fueled.[3] New blossoms will be produced, followed by new fruit.

The month of Shevat has a clear role in the natural cycle of the world. What is the spiritual root of this?

The Dissemination of Torah

A very special event occurred in Shevat:

And it was in the fortieth year, in the eleventh month [Shevat], on the first of the month...Moshe began to explain this Torah...
(Devarim 1:3–5)

It is interesting to note how the Torah describes Moshe's dissemination of the Torah: "Moshe began to explain [be'er] this Torah..." (Devarim 1:5). The word be'er means "well."

The Torah specifically highlights Shevat as the month in which Moshe began to transmit the book of Devarim, which reviews the laws enumerated in the previous four books of the Torah. This month is ripe for such an event. The dissemination of water to the trees is the physical manifestation of a spiritual force which produced the dissemination of this particular part of the Torah.[4] Let us examine this more closely.

Among the parallels between Torah and water that we discussed in "Cheshvan," there is one that especially concerns us here. The Midrash states that just as water brings life to the world, so does Torah bring life to those who study it.[5] Water is not just a requirement for life; it is a fundamental source of life at a physical level. It is water that brings life to nature. Water, in the form of rain, is the manifestation of a *chiyus*, a life force, being delivered to the world.

Torah is that *chiyus*. It is not merely another aspect of the life of a Jew — it is his life force. That which sustains man physically is water, but that which sustains him as a Jew is Torah. Torah is the essence of Judaism, the link between man and his Creator. In a broader context, the entire universe is sustained by the Torah. As the genetic material with which the universe was created, the Torah is the source and sustenance of the universe.

The *mazal* of Shevat is the *d'li,* the bucket that raises water up from the well. This is considered the *mazal* of the Jewish people.[6] Moshe is described by the daughters of Yisro as the one "who poured [*dalo*] the water for us,"[7] alluding to his role in disseminating the waters of Torah. Eliezer, the servant of Avraham, is described as one who poured out (*doleh*) from his master's Torah to others. In Shevat, we have the power of the *d'li* for disseminating Torah to the world.

The Tree of Torah

Shevat is the month in which the dissemination of rain begins the production of fruit in trees. And Shevat is the month in which the dissemination of Torah produces its own fruit.

It is a tree of life for those who support it.

(Mishlei 4:2)

Torah is not just life, it is called the "tree of life." Like a tree, it produces fruit. The Written Torah is the tree, and the Oral Torah is its fruit. Just as fruit are the offspring of a tree and draw their nourishment from it, so too is the Oral Torah the "offspring," the extension, of the Written Torah, and it draws its nourishment from it. By this we mean that the Written Torah provides the data which the Oral Torah examines, analyzes, and expounds.

The transition from the Written Torah to the Oral Torah is not abrupt. There is an intermediate stage, the book of Devarim. Although it is technically part of the Written Torah, in essence it is Oral Torah. With the first four books, Hashem Himself spoke from Moshe's mouth. But with the book of Devarim, Moshe acted as an agent for that which Hashem had told him.[8] The book of Devarim was developed with the involvement of man and is therefore essentially the beginning of the Oral Torah. Shevat, the beginning of the trees' fruit, is the beginning of the Torah's fruit. It is the month in which Moshe began to transmit the book of Devarim.[9]

Fruit and Vegetables

Tu BiShevat, the New Year for trees, is a time of great festivity. We may wonder, though, why this should be so. We do not find such celebration on the new year for vegetables or crops. What is so special about fruit?

A distinction between fruit and crops is found at the beginning of the Torah. In the utopia of Gan Eden, Adam was instructed that his diet would consist of fruit:[10]

And Hashem, God, commanded man, saying, "You shall eat from any tree in the garden."

(Bereishis 2:16)

When Adam sinned and fell from his lofty spiritual stature, his diet was also reduced to a lower status:

And to Adam He said, "...the land is cursed because of you; you shall eat in suffering all your life. It shall sprout thorns and thistles for you, and you shall eat the grasses of the field."

(Ibid. 3:17–18)

No longer would the fruits of the trees sustain man. Now he was to live off the grasses of the field — wheat, barley, and other grains and vegetables. Upon hearing this, Adam became greatly distressed:

"Rabbi Yehudah said: '[The tree from which Adam HaRishon ate] was wheat' " (Sanhedrin 70b). Before Adam's sin, wheat grew in the form of a fruit-bearing tree (Pri Tzaddik, Shevat 3; also based on Shabbos 30b).

When Hashem said to Adam, "*It shall sprout thorns and thistles for you...,*" his eyes streamed with tears; he said, "Master of the Universe! I and my donkey shall eat from a single trough!"

(*Pesachim* 118a)

In the transition from a diet of fruit to one of crops, Adam perceived that he had fallen to a status approaching that of an animal. In "Sivan" we contrasted the natures of man and animal. If we contrast fruit with crops and vegetables, we can see the same essential difference.[11]

More than Meets the Eye

When grains and vegetables are grown, the entire plant is cut and consumed. What you see is what you get. Once it is consumed, there is nothing left. There is never any further possibility of produce from this plant.

A fruit tree is different. What you see is only a tiny fraction of what you get. For even when all the fruit has been consumed, there remains vast potential in the tree. It has the ability to produce more fruit, and more, for many generations.

The sotah is considered to have performed the archetypal sin. The Gemara states that "a man does not sin unless a spirit of foolishness has entered him" (Sotah 3a) and learns this from the sotah. The Mishnah says, "Since she performed an animalistic act, she brings a korban of animal food" (Sotah 2:1). Giving in to one's bestial desires reflects the restricted spiritual potential characteristic of animals.

Adam was originally on the level of eating fruit. He was a vast reserve of potential waiting to be actualized. But when he sinned, he dropped to little more than the level of an animal. An animal has nothing more to it than meets the eye. It does not possess great potential that can be used for creative spiritual expression. It therefore subsists on a diet of crops and vegetables, which likewise have no potential for further development. In the same way, Adam's capacity for spiritual development was greatly reduced.

From Earth to Heaven

The conceptual difference between fruits and vegetables is also expressed in their contrasting appearances. Fruit trees stand tall, reaching upward from the earth toward the heavens. They represent a striving for spiritual growth and a potential that desires expression. Crops and vegetables, on the other hand, lie low to the ground; they represent lowly physicality and no desire for elevation.[12]

> Adam HaRishon reached from earth to Heaven...but when he sinned, Hashem laid His hand upon him and diminished him...
>
> (*Sanhedrin* 38b)

A corresponding decline in the quality of fruit also took place with the Destruction: "From the day the Beis HaMikdash was destroyed...the taste of fruit has been removed" (Sotah 48a).

This *gemara* is speaking in metaphorical terms which we can now understand.[13] Adam originally reached up toward the heavens like the fruit trees, expressing a tremendous potential for growth. But after the snake led him to sin, this potential became severely limited. The snake itself, which masterminded the sin, changed from being a creature that walked upright, paralleling the tree, to one that slithers in the dust, paralleling the crops and vegetables. Man, unlike other animals, still walks upright. Though man's greatness was reduced, he was still left with the potential to grow and even reclaim his original stature.

Wicked Grass and Righteous Trees

We find that righteous and wicked people are contrasted with the parallel of the unlimited potential of fruit trees versus the limits of crops:

> When the wicked flourish like grass, and the workers of iniquity sprout, it is to be destroyed forever.
>
> (Tehillim 92:8)

The sprouting of grasses (the early stage of the growth of grain) is followed by the consumption of the grain, leaving nothing behind. Similarly, the wicked may prosper in this world, but with no spiritual growth, they have no existence in the World to Come.[14]

> The righteous will flourish as the date palm... They still bring forth fruit in old age; they are fat and flourishing...
>
> (Ibid., 13–15)

The flourishing of the date palm means not only one harvest of fruit, but an annual supply, constantly increasing in size as the tree grows.[15] Similarly, righteous people enjoy the dividends of their spiritual labors in the long term.

"Happy is the man who does not walk with the advice of the wicked...but rather desires Hashem's Torah...and he shall be as a tree planted by streams of water, which gives its fruit in its season..." (Tehillim 1:1–3).

The Egyptian Donkey

In Adam HaRishon's cry of despair, he laments that he must eat the same food as his donkey. The donkey is called *chamor*, which is based on the word *chomer*, "material." The donkey is the most "materialistic" creature.[16] A simple-minded beast, it is drawn solely after its physical desires. Adam realized that his altered diet demonstrated a fall to such a level.

Interestingly, the donkey is linked with a particular nation:

> *In the land of Mitzrayim...whose flesh is as that of donkeys...*
> (Yechezkel 23:19–20)

The word chomer usually refers to a burden. Donkey is defined as "a beast of burden," the most menial task an animal can perform, as opposed to the agricultural tasks performed by oxen (Rabbi Shamshon Raphael Hirsch on Bereishis 12:16).

Mitzrayim was a nation steeped in materialistic drives and is therefore represented by the donkey.[17] It lacked any capacity for spiritual growth, and it is not surprising that the Jewish people remembered Mitzrayim as a land of vegetables:

> *We remember the fish we ate in Mitzrayim for nothing; the cucumbers, and the melons, and the leeks, and the onions, and the garlic...*
>
> (Bemidbar 11:5)

Vegetables, possessing none of the vast potential of fruit trees, express the essence of Mitzrayim.[18] And thus it is described when it is contrasted with Eretz Yisrael:

In contrast to the restrictive meitzarim of Mitzrayim, Eretz Yisrael is described as "a goodly and expansive land" (Shemos 3:8).

> *For the land which you are entering to possess is not like the land of Egypt which you left, where you sow your seeds and water it by walking [to bring water from the Nile], like a vegetable garden.*
> (Devarim 11:10–12)

The very name *Mitzrayim* is based on the word *meitzar*, "restriction," referring to its limited capacity for growth and lack of spiritual potential.

Winter, as we have noted, is the "exile" period of the year. But this section of winter is particularly connected to the exile in Mitzrayim. This is signified by the weekly Torah readings at this time, which discuss our exile in Egypt. Conceptually, then, we are at a "vegetable" stage, one that restricts spiritual growth. That is why the New Year of the fruit trees, with all its spiritual significance, is a cause of great celebration.

A View Ahead

The Exodus from Mitzrayim and the subsequent entry into Eretz Yisrael represent a transition from vegetables to fruit. Eretz Yisrael is essentially described as a land of fruit:

> *A land of wheat,*[19] *and barley, and vines, and figs, and pomegranates, a land of olive oil and [date] honey.*
>
> (Devarim 8:8)

If we look ahead, we see that this transition will be reflected in the development from Pesach to Shavuos.[20] On Pesach the *korban omer* is brought from barley, which is animal food. On Shavuos, two loaves of bread baked from wheat, food for humans, are brought. Thus, the spiritual growth of this period is represented by the development from animal (vegetable) status to human (fruit) status.

> At four times of year the world is judged: on Pesach for the grain, on Shavuos for the fruit of the tree...
>
> (*Rosh HaShanah* 1:2)

The first fruits begin to ripen on Shavuos. This process is paralleled to man; the spiritual perfection of Shavuos enables man to recover some of the fruit tree's potential. Shavuos transports us back to the giving of the Torah at Sinai, the day on which the Jewish people briefly returned to the level of Adam HaRishon before his sin.

> Rabbi Yehudah said in the name of Rabbi Akiva: "...Why did the Torah tell us to bring two loaves on Atzeres [Shavuos]? Because Atzeres is the time of the [first ripening of the] trees' fruit. Said Hashem: 'Bring two loaves of bread on Atzeres so that the fruit of the trees would be blessed.'"
>
> *(Rosh HaShanah 16a)*

> I heard that Rabbi Yehudah is going according to his reasoning, as he said in *Sanhedrin* (70b), that the tree from which Adam HaRishon ate was wheat.
>
> *(Rashi loc. cit.)*

Hope for the Future

It is not only memories of a time long gone that we can ponder. There are great times yet to come, times in which the trees will display their true glory:

> In the future, all the wild trees of Eretz Yisrael will bear fruit...
>
> *(Kesubos 112b)*

"Then all the trees of the forest shall rejoice" (Tehillim 96:12).

Those will be times in which we shall return to the level of Adam's original spiritual heights:

> In the future...trees will bear fruit every month, and man will eat of them and be healed...
>
> *(Shemos Rabbah 15:21)*

We yearn for the final redemption, through which we will regain the spiritual level of Adam in Gan Eden. Tu BiShevat is the day of rejoicing over fruit, the more spiritual of foods, and a day of hope for man's ultimate restoration to his true greatness.

Buds of Redemption

Shevat is the second to last month. The sequence of the year, which began with the bright blossoming of spring, is now drawing to a close. The countryside is silent, and everything is suppressed under the grip of winter. Nature looks more bleak than ever before.

And yet, deep down, life is beginning again. The harsh rains of winter are serving as fuel, in preparation for the new growth of spring. Just when things seem to be at their worst, a new cycle is in preparation. The trees are budding, and the sap has begun to rise inside them.

The days of my people are like the days of a tree.
(Yeshayahu 14:22)

So, too, is the situation of the Jewish people. At this time of year, we had not yet left Mitzrayim. Yet even as we are under the wintry suppression of Mitzrayim, we prepare to begin anew. The wellsprings of Torah develop us, the sap of life rises within us, preparing us for the fresh start of the new cycle of months, readying us for spring and for Pesach. This is the time to begin revitalizing ourselves in readiness for redemption.

Stems from the Source

What is it that enables a tree to survive the onslaught of winter? What is it that enables new leaves to grow when the previous ones were stripped off? What enables new twigs to sprout when the old twigs were destroyed by storms?

For there is hope for the tree — if it is cut down, it will sprout again, and its nourishment from the soil will not cease...

(Iyov 14:7)

The strength of the tree is not contained in their adornment of leaves, twigs, and branches. Its strength is in its inner core, which preserves the ability to continually draw nourishment from its source in the soil from which it grew.

Such is the case with the Jewish people. Material wealth and power, however spectacular they may appear to be, are transitory, lost in the stormy phases of history. If we were to bind ourselves solely to the material aspect of our lives, we would disappear along with all the other empires of the world. Our existence perpetuates only insofar as we attach ourselves to our Source, to our Creator. By drawing our lives from Hashem, we are able to survive even the harshest winter.[21]

However disconsolate the abandonment on earth may appear, the dedicated tenth remains, and even if it is repeatedly destroyed — like the oak and beech trees, which retain their stem while losing their leaves and twigs — so His stem remains for the future Sanctuary.

(Yeshayahu 6:12–13)

Toward Fruit

As we move from winter into spring, we celebrate the seasons of rejuvenation and renewal. The months of Shevat, Adar, and Nissan all rejoice in the revitalization of the trees and the plants. But during this joyful time, we must remember that we are not celebrating the general renewal of nature. We are celebrating its renewal insofar as it means that the cycle of fruit and crop production has begun, and eventually new fruit will be produced. We rejoice in the rejuvenation with our sights set firmly on its purpose. The revival of the trees and plants is a means to an end.

The same is true of the spiritual redemption that dawns at this time. The purpose of the Exodus in spring was not the liberation in itself, but rather the giving of the Torah on Har Sinai, the construction of the Mishkan, and the resting of the *Shechinah* among the Jewish people.[22] The ultimate goal of redemption is to further our relationship with Hashem.

ADAR

Nemesis

Adar is the twelfth and final month of the year. In the closing stages of late winter, we begin to set our sights on spring:

> *Guard the month of spring...*
>
> (Devarim 16:1)

The *beis din* looks ahead to spring in order to determine whether Pesach will occur then. If spring is still a little way off, they add another month to the year. (Nowadays we have a fixed calendar, with leap years occurring at set times during a nineteen-year cycle.)

We learned earlier (in the section "Solar Years," in the chapter "Dividing the Calendar") that the leap year is indicative of a spiritual struggle between Yaakov (the Jewish people) and Eisav (Rome; Western civilization). Eisav currently controls the material world, represented by the sun, while Yaakov engages in spiritual pursuits, represented by the moon. Enabling the lunar cycle to catch up with the solar cycle indicates the eventual harmonization between our spiritual task and our role in the material world. Eisav, who pursues domination in this world, ultimately loses it; Yaakov, who pursues spirituality, eventually triumphs in the material realm, too.

It is specifically Adar to which we add another month. The extra month is not considered a thirteenth month; it is rated as another department of the twelfth month.[1] Therefore, there are considered to be two Adars.

The *Tur* states that each month of the year is represented by one of the twelve tribes. Adar represents Yosef, who has a special ability to defeat Eisav:

And the house of Yaakov shall be fire, and the house of Yosef flame, and the house of Eisav shall be for stubble...

(Ovadiah 1:18)

Why does Eisav fall into the hands of Yosef?... Yosef grew up amidst two evil men, Poti Fera and Pharaoh, and did not learn from their evil ways; Eisav grew up amidst two righteous men and did not learn from their righteous ways... Eisav sullied himself with adultery and murder; Yosef guarded himself from adultery and murder... Eisav tried to kill his brother; Yosef fed and supported his brothers...

(*Pesikta Rabbasi* 12)

Perhaps this explains why the number thirteen, and especially the thirteenth of February (usually Adar), is viewed by non-Jews as unlucky.

Yosef is also unique in that he has the power of two tribes. The tribe of Yosef is often divided into the tribes of Efraim and Menasheh, his two sons: "Efraim and Menasheh shall be as Reuven and Shimon to me."[2] So the twelfth month, which represents Yosef, has the ability to become two months and conquer Eisav.[3]

The Hungry Bear

Adar is the month in which we celebrate Purim. Purim marks our victory over the kingdom of Persia and Media, led by Achashveirosh (coupled with Amalek, in the persona of Haman). These events were recorded in megillas Esther, and are well known to all.

In the Gemara, however, various Sages offer "keys" to the megillah, single verses from elsewhere in the Torah which express the essence of the entire episode (according to each Sage's perception). There is one in particular which concerns us:

> Reish Lakish opened up that episode based on this: *The lion roars, the bear growls, the wicked man rules over a poor nation* (Mishlei 28:15).
>
> *The lion roars* refers to Nevuchadnetzar...
>
> *The bear growls* refers to Achashveirosh, as it is written [in Daniel's dream, in reference to the kingdom of Persia], ...*and afterwards was an animal like a bear*, and Rabbi Yosef taught that this refers to the Persians, who eat and drink like a bear, and are clothed in flesh like a bear, and are hairy like a bear, and have no rest like a bear.
>
> *The wicked man rules* refers to Haman.
>
> *Over a poor people* refers to Yisrael, who were impoverished from mitzvos.
>
> (*Megillah* 11a)

The bear, the embodiment of the force of Persia,[4] was formerly a widespread creature. Israel's subspecies of the grizzly bear was known as the Syrian bear, and its last member was killed in Nachal Amud, near the Kinneret, in 1865.

Bears are highly dangerous creatures. Unlike other predators, such as lions and leopards, which attack only when hungry, bears are actually aggressive and kill people regularly. When the Torah describes an extremely dangerous enemy, it uses the bear as a metaphor: "It is better to meet a mother bear bereft of her cubs than a fool in his madness."[5] Bear cubs are astonishingly small, weighing only two hundred and fifty grams, and utterly helpless. The mother bear invests enormous effort into raising her cubs and forms an es-

"[Hashem] is to me like a bear lying in wait..." (Iyov 3:10) — this refers to the kingdom of Persia (Midrash Lekach Tov loc. cit.).

pecially close bond with them.[6] She is therefore a particularly protective mother and a highly dangerous foe. The males are vicious, too, in their fight with other bears to secure a mate. With their poor eyesight, they may often confuse a person with another bear.

The Gemara explains that the bear represents Persia in terms of its ravenousness. Bears eat almost anything — not only herbage and fish, but also grubs, rodents, carrion, and livestock. This diet results in their massive bulk, weighing up to six hundred pounds.

The Persian empire expanded ravenously, engulfing all. They continually fought and conquered, never satisfied: "They have no rest, like a bear [which wanders constantly in search of food]." On an individual level, they were steeped in hunger and desire: "They eat and drink like a bear."[7] Achashveirosh's enormous feast demonstrated their preoccupation with pursuing their desires. Such was the evil of Persia.

" 'As when a man flees from a lion and is met by a bear...' (Amos 5:19) — the bear is Media" (Pesikta D'Esther Rabbah 5).

Bear Surprise

Each of the four creatures in Daniel's dream manifests a different type of evil. The ferocity represented by the bear is used against the Jewish people in a specific situation.

Exile is a period of banishment during which the Jewish people are not able to live in Eretz Yisrael and fulfill all the mitzvos. This is supposed to be an unsatisfactory state of affairs for the Jewish people, one that spurs them to improve their observance of the Torah and merit redemption.

Unfortunately, people sometimes miss the point. They do not miss having a Beis HaMikdash, and they feel no stimulus to improve their ways. They relax in exile and feel comfortable. But if we go down to *galus* this way, we are in for a big surprise. For it is against this sort of complacency that the bear is sent.

The first example of this concerns Yosef, when he was exiled from his father's house. As a slave in Mitzrayim, with his father mourning his presumed death, he was not supposed to be content with his state of affairs. But as he rose in position to be the controller

of his master Poti Fera's affairs, he became complacent about his lifestyle:

> *Yosef was beautiful of form and appearance* (Bereishis 39:6) — since he saw himself as a ruler, he began eating and drinking and curling his hair. Hashem said: "Your father is in mourning and you are curling your hair? I will set the bear upon you!" Immediately, *his master's wife lifted her eyes toward Yosef, and she said, "Lie with me..."*
>
> (Bereishis Rabbah 87:3)

The bear is always wandering[8] and has no rest, says the Gemara. Such is supposed to be the lot of the Jew in exile. If the Jew considers himself at rest, then the bear is sent to remind him otherwise.

"And now they sin more and more... I am Hashem your God... When they were fed, they became full; they were filled, and they became high-spirited; therefore they have forgotten me... I will meet them like a bear which is bereft of her cubs, and I will tear open their closed hearts..."
(Hoshea 13:2–8).

So, too, was the situation at the time of Achashveirosh. The Jews indulged themselves in his feast, ignoring their position in exile. Their complacency called for an attack by the bear. Sure enough, Achashveirosh turned against them and sealed a decree to annihilate them. It was only when they returned to Hashem through fasting and prayer that the decree was rescinded. We finally learned the lesson that the Jew in exile is to view his situation as strictly temporary and yearn for redemption.

House of the Hyrax

The hyraxes are not a strong people... — this refers to Media.

And they put their homes among the rocks — this refers to Achashveirosh and Koresh, who wanted to build the Beis HaMikdash.

(Midrash Mishlei 30:26)

The Midrash[9] notes some further parallels:

- The hyrax possesses one kosher sign, that of chewing its cud, and one non-kosher sign, that of not having a true hoof. With similar unevenness, Persia and Media would produce both righteous and wicked people.

- Just as the hyrax is *ma'aleih geirah*, "raises up its cud," so did Persia raise up its voice in praise of Hashem: "So says Koresh, king of Persia: 'Hashem, the God of the Heavens, has given me all of the rulership of the lands, and He has appointed me to build Him a house, in Yerushalayim, which is in Judea.' "[10]

- Just as the hyrax brings up its cud, so did Persia and Media "bring up" (i.e., form an environment in which was created) a *tzaddik* — Mordechai.

- The hyrax is *ma'aleih geirah*, "brings up its cud." So, too, Persia and Media dragged (*megarer*, based on the word *geirah*) another kingdom after them — Yavan.

The Pig Pretends

In "Av" we noted that the pig represents Edom, the legacy of Eisav. One explanation of this is given in the Midrash:

Why is the pig called *chazir*? Because it is destined to re-turn [*lehachazir*] the crown of splendor to Yisrael.

(Vayikra Rabbah 13:5)

At face value, this *midrash* indicates that the relationship of the pig to Edom is based on the etymology of its name alone. But this cannot be. Somehow, the word *chazir* must relate to the very essence of the pig and Edom.

Let us first explore another parallel between the two evils noted by the Midrash. Most animals bend their legs at the knee when lying down, folding them beneath their bodies. Not so the pig — it stretches its legs straight out in front of it. In doing so, it is trying to cover up for the fact that it does not chew its cud; it is advertising that it possesses cloven hooves. "Look, I'm kosher!" says the pig. And outwardly, such appears to be the case. But the inner workings of the animal prove otherwise. Try as it might to attain the status of animals that return (*machazir*) their cud to their mouths, the pig falls short.

In the same way, Edom claims to be the kosher nation. Under the banner of Christianity, they assert themselves as the new chosen people. They claim to be the champions of truth and justice. In fact, not only are they not the new chosen people, but they are also guilty of the most wicked crimes behind a veneer of uprightness. To pick but one example, the Crusades are advanced as noble Christians trying to bring religious morality to wicked Moslem infidels. But as we know only too well, the Crusades were an excuse for the Christians to terrorize their way through Europe, burning large numbers of Jews at the stake on the way.

This tradition of presenting a false facade of righteousness was initiated by Eisav, the ancestor of Edom. He would ask his father, Yitzchak, how to tithe salt, knowing full well that it does not require tithing.[11] In doing so, he was trying to present himself as a kosher son, instead of the villain he actually was.

Edom is the last and most terrible of the evil empires to rise up against us. The pretense of being better than us is the last card, so to speak, that the nations play against us. It's not a matter of "If you can't beat them, join them"; it's more like "If you can't beat them, *be* them." When Edom rose to power, and claimed to be the new chosen people, it was a sign that the chain of exiles was nearing the end. Thus, the pig, which pretends to be kosher and tries to emulate those creatures which are *machazir* their cud to their mouths, fundamentally relates to Edom, whose pretense of being the real chosen people is a sure sign that they are soon to return the crown of splendor to us.

Just as the pig stretches out its legs and pretends to be kosher, so too did Eisav entice women away from their husbands, and when he reached the age of forty, he pretended to be like his father and said, "My father married at forty; so shall I!" (Bereishis Rabbah 65:1).

Purim, the day of victory over Haman, is the day of downfall for Amalek and, by extension, Edom. Their policy of pretending to be something that they are not, for evil purposes, is destroyed on this day. That being the case, we have an insight into an aspect of Purim. We are instructed that "if anyone stretches out their hand [for charity], give to them [without checking to see if they are genuinely needy or out to steal]."[12] The phrase used for stretching out the hand, *poshet yad*, is identical to that used to describe the pig's display of its cloven hooves. Edom pretends to be kosher for evil purposes. On Purim, the day of Edom's downfall, that power is annulled. On Purim, no one pretends to be something they are not for evil purposes. If anyone stretches out their hand, we must give them charity.[13]

Cooling Off

We are now at the furthest time of year from last Nissan, from the last spring sun. The memory of the unique closeness we shared with Hashem at that time, the special perception of His control, has begun to lose its sharpness and clarity. The long, bleak winter has taken its toll on us; the season of *kor* tries to cool down our fiery soul.

This, the end of the year, is when the threat of Amalek occurs. In *parashas Zachor*, which we read at this time, we are told:

> *Remember what Amalek did to you, when he happened across you [karcha] on the way...*
>
> (Devarim 25:18)

The word *karcha* is based on the word *mikreh*, "happen," and on the root *kor*, "cold."[14] Haman, a descendant of Amalek, tried to destroy us in Adar, the time of year furthest from Nissan and Pesach. For in Nissan we lived through the Exodus, the time of Hashem's clear and open salvation, revealed for all to see. We glow with our connection to Divine assistance; we burn with excitement at our task as Hashem's people. This is what Amalek wants to attack. He cools us down, trying to make us forget, to become hazy about Hashem's role in the world.

How does he do this? His tool is reflected in the other meaning of *karcha*, "happen." Amalek tells us that there is no higher purpose to the events of this world, they just "happen" that way. He tells us that Hashem does not control the world; there is just a naturally random course of events. Even more dangerously, Amalek is not swayed by the unique events of history. They say that they were all just coincidences;

besides, you don't want to get involved with all that heavy religious stuff — "chill out!" The universe is governed by chance, Amalek says, with no Divine guidance and no possibility of Divine intervention.

The threat of extinction at the hands of Haman was a resultant effect of succumbing to their ideology. We lost sight of the unique role we had been entrusted with by Hashem. We decided that we could decrease persecution from the Persians by befriending them, and we thus flocked to the feast of Achashveirosh. We lost interest in the fact that the rules which govern the Jewish people are not the standard rules which govern the rest of mankind. Hashem guides us directly and gives us special instructions on how to relate to the nations of the world. Hashem tells us that assimilation won't get us anywhere. But we had cooled off from that idea, relaxing in the fantasy that there is no Divine guidance.

Eventually we repented, following Mordechai's advice. The Jewish people fasted for three days, proving that they believed their fate to rest solely in Hashem's hands. When they did this, Hashem brought about our salvation in a way that totally refuted the Amalekite ideology, through a subtle and ingenious method. Rather than use open miracles, Hashem guided "chance" events to bring about a victory. And it was a victory that would have looked absolutely impossible from the outset. The prime minister hanged? The Jews killing their enemies rather than the other way around? Inconceivable! And yet it came about, not through lightning bolts and plagues, but through a subtle manipulation of events. This showed that even "chance" events do not just "happen" that

"It is analogous to a boiling bathtub which no one can enter, and one wicked one comes and jumps inside; though he is scalded, he cools it down for others. So too here; the children of Yisrael left Mitzrayim, and Hashem split the sea for them and drowned the Egyptians in it. Fear of them fell upon the nations of the world...but when Amalek came to intercept them, even though they received what they deserved, they cooled down [the children of Yisrael] for the rest" (Midrash Tanchuma, Ki Seitzei 9).

way, but that everything is Divinely orchestrated.

This is the threat of *kor*, and this is the key to salvation. We must hold on to the heights we reached in Nissan and not let the forces of Amalek cool us down. It must be absolutely clear to us that Hashem directly controls everything that happens in the world. Not a blade of grass grows without Hashem saying so. We have a unique role in history we must try our utmost to live up to. We must not "chill out"; we must remain "fired up"!

Awakenings

Haman said to King Achashveirosh, "There is a certain people [yeshno am echad] scattered and dispersed among the people..."
(Esther 3:8)

The one called "echad" [Hashem] is sleeping [yoshein].
(*Esther Rabbah* 7:12)

The people were "sleeping" [yesheinim] from mitzvos.
(*Midrash Panim Acheirim* 1)

In the thick of winter, nature sleeps. In Shushan, the Jews also succumbed to "sleep," performing mitzvos by rote, with lethargy and lack of conviction. Reflecting our approach, Hashem went into "sleep" mode, leaving the world on "autopilot." He allowed Amalek, the presenters of the natural system of events, to take control.

But when the Jews repented and began to perform mitzvos actively, with conviction, Hashem responded in turn:

On that night, the king's sleep was disturbed...
(Esther 6:1)

We are taught that although, simply speaking, the

king spoken of in the megillah is Achashveirosh, at a deeper level it alludes to the true King, Hashem. When the Jews began to perform mitzvos with enthusiasm and zeal, Hashem "awoke" and began to interfere with the course of events, bringing salvation.[15]

As spring dawns, nature begins to wake up. The animals emerge from hibernation. The earth sprouts new life. We, too, must try to put new life into our service of Hashem. We must strive to perform mitzvos with zest and enthusiasm, waking up along with nature.

The Sprouting of Joy

As new plant growth begins to sprout forth from the ground, a mood of expansiveness fills the air. Mirroring the *teshuvah* out of awe in Elul, we now engage in *teshuvah* out of love. As the growing plants move outward, so do we move toward Hashem with love, in anticipation of the renewal of spring that approaches.

The צמיחה (*tzemichah*), "sprouting," demonstrated by the plants also relates to the שמחה (*simchah*), "joy," of this month.[16] Joy is a result of expansiveness, the awareness of inner life surging forth.[17] Another word for "joy" is *gilah*, which also means "reveal." When a person's inner happiness is revealed, when it is radiated by his whole being, that is true joy.

The Dawning of Redemption

One of the remarkable aspects of the Purim victory was that it came from totally unexpected areas. That is, it was precisely those events that caused the trouble which eventually brought about our salvation.

A case in point is the feast of Achashveirosh. This was the cause of Haman's rise to power, as it was then that he successfully advised Achashveirosh how to deal with Vashti's refusal to appear. The feast thus brought about the appointment of a deadly enemy to prime minister. At a deeper level, the feast caused the forces of Amalek to have power over us. Trying to combat hatred with assimilation meant succumbing to Amalekite ideology and condemning ourselves to destruction. Surely the feast marks a black point in our history.

"God is our refuge and strength, a help to be greatly found in trouble" (Tehillim 46:2). It is precisely from within the trouble that Hashem's help comes.

And yet, when we repented, our salvation resulted from that very same feast. Not only that, but it was specifically that occurrence that enabled Haman to rise to power which brought about our victory.

How did Haman win favor with the king? Through advising him to dispose of Vashti. And who was Vashti's replacement? Esther, who persuaded the king to spare the Jewish people and hang Haman. The same feast which brought about the threat of our destruction brought about our victory. We see very clearly that something can appear to be very bad, even catastrophic, and yet contain within it the potential for endless good.

As the summer passes, changes begin to occur in nature. The trees begin to shed their leaves. Flowers and plants wither, falling to the ground. Underground, the seeds seemingly begin to decompose, disintegrating among the soil. Then the shining sun is covered by dark clouds. Rain pours in torrents from the sky, battering all it encounters. Storms and winds rage; blizzards cover all with snow. The countryside appears to have been completely destroyed.

And yet spring follows. More than that — it was the seemingly terrible winter which enabled the spring to come. For how can life rejuvenate without the rains of winter? How can there be room for new growth, more luxuriant growth, without the old growth stripped away? That which appeared to be the end of the world is now seen to be the cause for its revitalization.

For behold, the winter has passed; the rain is over and gone. The shoots appear in the ground...

(Shir HaShirim 2:11–12)

This parallels the Jewish people. Just as the rains cause the new growth to sprout, so too do our troubles cause us to repent and bring about salvation. We have seen that not only are the troubles eventually followed by salvation, but they were the cause of salvation all along.[18]

This is the message of Purim, and of Adar. And this is the cause of the tremendous *simchah* of this month. It is the elation of seeing how everything that seemed to be so terrible turned out to be for the best after all. It is the *simchah* we will feel at the time of the final redemption, when we will see how two thousand years of bitter exile were the cause of salvation and Mashiach.

אז ימלא שחק פינו ולשוננו רנה...

Then our mouths will be full of laughter and our tongues with glad song...

(Tehillim 126:2)

"Rabbi Shimon bar Nachmani opened up that episode based on the verse 'In place of the thorn, the cypress has come up, and in place of the nettles, the myrtle has come up' (Yeshayahu 55:13). In place of Haman, Mordechai has triumphed, and in place of Vashti, Esther has triumphed" (Megillah 10b). It was precisely from the source of evil that good emerged.

Perhaps the cypress signifies the approach of the stork, the bird that heralds salvation, which "makes its home in the cypresses" (Tehillim

תם ונשלם
שבח לא-ל בורא עולם

AFTERWORD

This is not the end.

We continue through time, with Nissan and spring harvest. As the sprouting of salvation takes place, we experience the renewal of Rosh Chodesh Nissan. We wake up from the darkness of winter exile to the light of rejuvenation, to the spring of redemption.

NOTES

INTRODUCTION

1. *Chovos HaLevavos, Sha'ar HaBechinah,* Introduction.

2. *Chovos HaLevavos, Sha'ar HaBechinah.* Compare, however, the *Tzlach* on *Berachos* 28b, which states that this was true only in the time of Rabbeinu Bachya (eleventh century), but that nowadays studying the universe leads people away from Hashem. Nevertheless, it would seem that *this* was true only in his time (nineteenth century). His reason is that people were being taught that everything is deterministic and can be traced to natural causes, leaving no room for a Creator. Since then, science has learned, in fields such as quantum physics and chaos theory, that *nothing* is deterministic, that it is impossible to ever fully know the universe. Additionally, there have been many scientific discoveries which point toward a Creator, notably the discovery that the universe itself had a beginning. (See Appendix A.)

3. *Chovos HaLevavos, Sha'ar HaBechinah,* ch. 2.

4. See *Chovos HaLevavos, Sha'ar HaBechinah,* Introduction, which states that people lack both knowledge of the benefits of Hashem's universe and appreciation of that which they do know. He blames the latter in part on people taking for granted the benefits they grew up with.

5. Similarly, Rambam, in *Sefer HaMitzvos,* mitzvah 3, states: "That which He commanded us regarding loving Him; and this means that we should think and contemplate His mitzvos, utterances, and actions..." There seems, however, to be a difficulty with this. In the aforementioned *Hilchos Yesodei HaTorah* (2:2) Rambam speaks only of contemplating the natural world and makes no mention of contemplating the beauty of Torah. *Kinas Sofrim* explains simply that Rambam in *Hilchos Yesodei HaTorah* is discussing only the physical world

and is not dealing with Torah, the concepts of which are discussed in *Hilchos Talmud Torah*. Rabbi Yitzchak Hutner, in *Pachad Yitzchak* (Shavuos 23), questions Rambam in *Hilchos Yesodei HaTorah* from this *Sifri* and resolves them by distinguishing between different stages of love — the inital desire to draw close to Hashem is triggered by contemplating the beauty of the natural world, but this yearning to know Him is fulfilled only through studying Torah.

Rabbi Shamshon Raphael Hirsch states in the third letter of *The Nineteen Letters* (Feldheim Publishers, 1995) that the Torah is to be used as the guide to correctly understanding the natural world (see extensive notes by Rabbi Joseph Elias). *Ibn Ezra* and *Malbim* on Tehillim, ch. 19, demonstrate that affirming Hashem's existence from the Torah is preferable to deriving it from the natural world.

6. *Ibn Ezra* and *Malbim* on Tehillim, ch. 19.

7. *Radak* and *Malbim* on Tehillim, ch. 19.

8. *Nefesh HaChaim* 1:5.

9. Ibid. 2:5.

10. Ibid. 4:10.

11. Ibid., 28.

12. Ibid., 27.

13. This pattern is described by Rabbi Yehoshua Honigwachs in his book *The Unity of Torah* (Feldheim Publishers, 1991).

14. *Nefesh HaChaim* 4:10.

15. *Ramban*, Introduction to his commentary on the Torah.

CONCEPTS OF TIME

1. *Michtav MeEliyahu*, vol. 1, p. 103; vol. 2, p. 21.

2. Curiously, the word *zeman* appears in *Tanach* only in the books of Esther, Koheles, Daniel, Ezra, and Nechemiah. In every instance, it is written only in reference to preappointed times. But this is the word we use to refer to the concept of time in general. This indicates that all moments of time are predisposed to different activities.

3. Cf. Maharal, *Gevuros Hashem* 51.

4. Maharal, *Gevuros Hashem* 46.

5. *Ramban* on Vayikra 23:40.

6. *Michtav MeEliyahu*, vol. 1, p. 103; vol. 2, p. 21.

7. See *Pri Tzaddik*, Rosh Chodesh Menachem Av 1.

8. See Bereishis 19:3.

9. See Shemos 12:15.

10. Cf. *Beis HaLevi, parashas Bo.*

11. Devarim 16:1.

12. Shemos 23:15.

13. Ibid., 16.

14. Ibid. 34:22.

15. However, even countries with the same general climate as Eretz Yisrael lack its unique composition of flora and fauna, the significance of which is discussed later in the book.

16. *Derech Hashem*, pt. 2, ch. 7: "*Hashpa'as HaKochavim.*"

17. *Nedarim* 32a.

18. *Shabbos* 156a.

19. *Bnei Yissachar*, Shevat; see also *Rabbeinu Bachya* on Devarim 31:16.

20. *Shabbos* 156a.

SELECTING A CALENDAR

1. Shemos 12:2.

2. Reb Tzadok, *Likutei Ma'amarim.*

3. Ibid.

4. *Sifsei Chaim*, vol. 2, p. 264.

5. *Kenaf Renanim* on *Perek Shirah*, "Song of the Moon."

6. Bereishis 27:40.

7. Rabbi Shamshon Raphael Hirsch, *The Jewish Year*, "Adar II."

DIVIDING THE CALENDAR

1. On *Rosh HaShanah* 27a.

2. *Sifsei Chaim*, vol. 2, p. 167.

3. Shemos 12:2.

4. *Michtav MeEliyahu*, vol. 1, p.13.

5. Rabbi Shamshon Raphael Hirsch, *The Jewish Year*, "Tishrei I."

6. Cf. *Rashi* on Devarim 29:12, s.v. *"hayom."*

7. "With *kodshim*, night follows day," e.g., *Chullin* 83a; cf. *Rashi* on Devarim 29:12, s.v. *"hayom."*

8. Rambam, *Hilchos De'os* 1:4.

9. The only extreme point in the country is the Dead Sea, a body of water so saturated with salt and other minerals that nothing can live in it, but that is due to the Divine punishment of Sedom.

10. One might ask that Shavuos ought to therefore be in spring, not summer. The Maharal, in *Gevuros Hashem* 46, explains that the Torah does not give a date on which to celebrate Shavuos; we are simply told to celebrate it fifty days after Pesach, thereby linking it to Pesach and spring.

11. Maharal, *Gevuros Hashem* 46; *Netzach Yisrael* 8.

12. *Rashi*, based on *Bava Metzia* 106b; see also *Gur Aryeh*. Ibn Ezra counts four, considering *zera* and *katzir* to be more general divisions.

13. There is a three-way argument as to how the seasons are synchronized with the months (see *Bava Metzia* 106b). The simplest explanation has been chosen here. The synchronization of the seasons with the months is not absolutely precise, as the seasons are solar-based and the months are lunar-based.

14. *Rashi* on Bereishis 8:22.

15. Shemos 12:2.

16. *Bnei Yissachar, ma'amarei Nissan* 1, Introduction.

17. *Yerushalmi, Rosh HaShanah* 2:1.

18. *Bnei Yissachar, Ma'amarei Nissan* 1:6.

19. *Ramban* on Shemos 12:2.

20. See Yechezkel 8:14.

21. *Emes L'Yaakov*, Shemos 12:2. For an alternative explanation, see *Pri Tzaddik*, Rosh Chodesh Kislev 2.

22. Some think otherwise: "A number of body-clock watchers believe we also tick to an array of weekly cycles. These regulate changes in body chemicals, the response pattern of the immune system, and a cyclic rise and fall of heartbeat and blood circulation" (John Boslough, "The Enigma of Time," *National Geographic*, March 1990). But these may well be a *result* of the Shabbos-based weekly cycle.

23. Shemos 20:8; *Rabbeinu Bachya* on Shemos 12:2.

24. *Malbim* on Bereishis 8:22.

25. E.g., see Vayikra 25:2.

26. *Derech Hashem*, pt. 4, 7:2.

PATTERNS AND ELEMENTS

1. See *Ben Yehoyada* on *Ta'anis* 6b–7b.

2. Cf. *Ta'anis* 9b.

3. *Aderes Eliyahu*, Bereishis 2:6.

4. This is cited from *Pirkei D'Rabbi Eliezer*; cf. *Yalkut Shimoni* on Bereishis 2:6.

5. Based on *Bereishis Rabbah* 12:8, where it is stated slightly differently.

6. *Parashas Derachim*, *derush* 21.

7. Vayikra 26:4; see *Rashi* there.

8. See *Rashi*.

9. See *Seforno, Rashbam, Rosh, Da'as Zekeinim*, and *Chizkuni* on Devarim 11:10–12.

10. Maharal, *Ner Mitzvah* 1.

11. Maharal, *Netzach Yisrael* 55.

12. *Vayikra Rabbah* 13:5. As well as the non-kosher animals paralleling the exiles, it seems that the non-kosher birds parallel them, too. The first verse to describe non-kosher birds lists three species, the first of which is the *nesher*, "eagle" or "vulture." In Daniel's vision, Bavel was represented by a lion with the wings of a *nesher*. The second bird listed is the *paras*, a species of raptor, the name of which is identical to *Paras*, "Persia," the second exile. (This cannot be mere co-incidence; a name relates to the fundamental nature of the thing.) The third bird is the *azniah*, an osprey or similar species, so named because it possesses the trait of *azus*, "brazenness." As we shall learn in "Kislev," *azus* strongly relates to Yavan, the third exile. Edom does not appear to be in this sequence of birds.

13. The camel's hooves are reduced, such that they are closer to being nails. Camels are unique in that only the edges of their hooves touch the ground; the animal's weight rests on the sole-pads.

14. There seems to be little doubt concerning the identification of *shafan* as the hyrax, though many of the commentaries are wary of being definitive about

an animal for which there is no *masorah* (tradition) concerning its identity. The factors involved in this identification are as follows:

- The name *shafan* means "hidden one." Similarly, in Tehillim (104:18) we find the phrase "The rocks are a refuge for the *shefanim*." Hyraxes (the Israeli species, *procavia syriaca*, is called the rock hyrax) always live in rocky areas, in which they have a multitude of tunnels and hiding places. When danger threatens, they all dart into hiding.

- Although hyraxes do not ruminate in the proper, zoological sense of the term, they do approximate this behavior very closely. They have a complex gut, with three separate areas of microbial digestion, and they have an ability to digest fiber similar to that of true ruminants. According to several opinions, this qualifies for the Torah's description of *ma'aleih geirah*, "chewing the cud" (Vayikra 11:5).

- Hyraxes do not have true hooves, split or otherwise. However, their feet are of a peculiarly rubbery texture, and the hind feet possess only three closely joined toes. The Malbim sees this as perfectly described in the words of the verse: "*u'farsah lo yafris*" (ibid.). The precise meaning of this phrase (as contrasted with that describing the camel and the hare) is that it does not form hooves on its front feet, even though it has something approximating hooves on its hind feet.

- In Tehillim (104:18), the hyraxes are described immediately after the ibex (a species of wild goat). This may suggest geographical proximity, and both species are noticeably abundant in the hills surrounding the Dead Sea.

- "The *shefanim* are a small people, not strong" (Mishlei 30:26). Hyraxes, which measure only about fifteen inches long, are preyed upon by eagles, jackals, hyenas, and snakes.

- There may be a historical reason for identifying *shafan* as "hyrax." Historians say that three thousand years ago Phoenician sailors explored the Mediterranean, sailing westward from their homeland on the coast of Syria. They found land where they saw many animals they thought were hyraxes (but which subsequently turned out to be rabbits), and so they called the place *Ishaphan*, "Island of the Hyrax." The Romans later modified the name to Hispania, and we now know it as Spain.

- The identification of the *shafan* as the rabbit in certain translations of the *Chumash* is highly problematic. First, there are no rabbits in Israel, and the verses in Tehillim indicate that the *shafan* does exist in Israel. Second, the rabbit is so similar to the hare that it is difficult to imagine that the Torah would identify it separately from the *arneves*; the Torah's classification of animals is usually less specific than that of current zoology. The translation as the rock-badger or coney is vague, as both are generic terms covering a variety of animals.

At this point it is worth commenting on the popular zoological description of the hyrax. Reference works on the subject smugly inform that despite the external appearance of a hyrax resembling that of a guinea pig, their closest relatives are actually elephants. This rather surprising "fact" is based on certain similarities between hyraxes and elephants in their dental structure. The information is usually accompanied by an evolutionary tree depicting a hyrax-like animal as a common ancestor of both species, followed by a larger creature called *Moeritherium* as the intermediary stage to the elephant. The entire picture is presented as an example of the fossil record "proving" evolution. However, Sylvia Sikes, in *The Natural History of the Elephant* (Weidenfeld and Nicolson [London, 1971], pp. 2–4), points out that "it requires extreme elasticity of the imagination to see anything more than a very superficial resemblance between the available parts of the skeletons of the earliest hyraces and those of the Proboscidea (elephants)... In the light of recent comparative studies on the anatomy, physiology, ecology, and ethology of the living members of these orders, it is apparent that in the past disproportionate weight was sometimes given to skeletal affinities, while other important characteristics were overlooked... Perhaps we should admit that the siting of Moeritherium in an intermediate position in the family tree *savors more of the artistic requirements of the drawing board than of an honest admission of ignorance as to its proper position*." (Emphasis added.)

15. Identifying the *arneves* as "hare" is proposed by many commentaries but questioned by others. Nevertheless, it does seem to be correct, based on the following factors:

    - The name *arneves* is based on the words *ar*, "split," and *niv*, "lip" (*HaKesav V'HaKabbalah, parashas Shemini*). The upper lip of a hare is split in two. (Hence, humans born with such a feature are termed "hare-lipped.")

    - Although the hare does not properly ruminate, they do something very similar. In order to digest their food properly, much of it has to be passed through the gut twice. They therefore excrete soft pellets in the small hours of the morning (the significance of this time is discussed in "Kislev"and "Teves"), which they promptly consume. According to several opinions, this qualifies for the term *ma'aleih geirah* in the Torah.

- Hares do not, of course, possess any form of hoof. The Malbim notes that the phrase *"u'farsah lo hifrisah"* in the Torah (Vayikra 11:6), when understood according to the precision of the wording, means exactly that.

- When the Greeks ordered the sages to translate the Torah, they did not want to translate *arneves*, as that was the name of the queen, and they would be accused of mockery. Therefore, says the Gemara, they translated *arneves* as "short-legs," because its forelegs are much smaller than its back legs, as Rashi explains. This description matches the hare perfectly.

16. *Nesher* is traditionally taken to represent the eagle, of which there are several species in Eretz Yisrael. However, *Tosafos* (on *Chullin* 61a) disputes this identification, because the eagle possesses a large central toe. This is one of the four signs of a kosher bird, and it is stated that the *nesher* does not possess any of the signs of a kosher bird. Additionally, the *nesher* is described as being bald (Michah 1:18), and such a description only fits certain species of vulture (the bald eagle is not bald; it merely has white feathers on its head). Possibly, *nesher* is a generic term referring to both vultures and eagles; see Rabbi Dovid Brown, *Mysteries of Creation* (Targum Press, 1997) for a discussion on species classification. See also the *Beis Yosef* on *Yoreh De'ah* 82.

17. Or, alternatively, a wolf (see *Vayikra Rabbah* 13:5).

ROSH CHODESH

1. *Kenaf Renanim* on *Perek Shirah*; see also *Rabbeinu Yonah* on *Berachos* 21a.

2. Tehillim, ch.104.

3. *Tur, Hilchos Rosh Chodesh* 1.

4. For a full discussion about the identification of the *shafan* as the hyrax, see n. 14 to the chapter "Patterns and Elements."

5. *Rosh HaShanah* 26b; see *Me'iri* loc. cit.

6. *Midrash Tehillim* 104:18; *Rashi* and *Radak* on Tehillim 104:18; *Bereishis Rabbah* 12:8.

7. One may still wonder why Hashem created ibex to require this particular type of environment. This is a separate question, beyond our understanding. We

suggest a simple reason as follows: Man requires a large, curved shofar for certain fast days. Ibex were created to provide for that need. Such enormous horns make it impossible for them to escape from predators if there are any trees or bushes around; their horns would snag. Therefore, they need to have a rocky terrain which they can negotiate better than their predators.

8. *Tur*, citing *Pirkei D'Rabbi Eliezer* 42. There is a difficulty with this: the sin of the golden calf took place on the seventeenth of Tamuz — what connection does this have to Rosh Chodesh? The answer is that on that day the intentions of the women were not clear. Perhaps they were holding on to their jewelry for selfish reasons. The refutation of this came on Rosh Chodesh, when they gave their jewelry for the construction of the Mishkan. This proved that they had no selfish attachment to their jewelry, and their refusal to give it for the golden calf was based on their dedication to Hashem.

9. Cited by Jerry Dennis, *It's Raining Frogs and Fishes* (New York: Harper Collins Publishers, Inc., 1992), p. 231.

10. *Rema* 426:2.

11. Cf. *Ramban* on Bereishis 38:29.

12. *Maharsha*.

13. *Shemos Rabbah* 15.

14. Maharal, in many places, such as *Nesivos Olam*, p.142.

NISSAN

1. *Rosh HaShanah* 10b, according to Rabbi Yehoshua.

2. *Metzudas David*, Yeshayahu 61:11.

3. Yirmeyahu 33:15, according to *Metzudas David* and *Radak*.

4. *Sefer HaShorashim*.

5. *Gevuros Hashem* 3.

6. *Gevuros Hashem* 36, 51; cf. *Michtav MeEliyahu*, vol. 1, p. 117.

7. *Menachos* 41b; see also Rabbi Shamshon Raphael Hirsch on *tzitzis* in *Jewish Symbolism*.

8. Quoted in *Birkas Chaim*.

9. *Kenaf Renanim* on *Perek Shirah*.

10. *Gevuros Hashem* 36, 51.

11. *Sefer HaShorashim.*

12. Cf. *Sifsei Chaim*, vol. 1, p. 93.

13. *Gittin* 57a, apparently quoting Daniel 11:16.

14. *Yoma* 21a.

15. Ibid.

16. Ibid.

17. *Gevuros Hashem* 51. See the chapter on Tishrei in this book for a discussion on how time warps at that stage of the year.

18. *Or Gedalyahu, Mo'adim, Parashas HaChodesh* 3.

19. *Rashi* on Tehillim 65:14.

20. The significance of speech to Pesach perhaps gives an insight into tractate *Pesachim*, which begins with the words "On the light [eve] of the fourteenth we search for *chametz*," when it would be more accurate to write, "the *night* of the fourteenth." The commentaries explain that it is important to use positive rather than negative words in descriptions. With that which we have learned, we can understand why this is the very first lesson that begins tractate *Pesachim*.

21. *Tosafos*, Sanhedrin 37b.

22. *Or Gedalyahu, sefer Shemos, Beshalach* 3.

23. *Shemos Rabbah* 23:3.

24. *Sefas Emes* 5653.

25. *Gevuros Hashem* 47; *Sifsei Chaim*, vol. 2, "*Shirah*: Recognition of Unity."

26. *Or Gedalyahu, Mo'adim*, p. 143.

27. We are identifying *tzvi* as the gazelle and *ayal* as the deer. This is based on two factors. The *gemara* in *Chullin* 59b states that the *tzvi* does not have branched antlers (see *Rashi*, who therefore identifies it as a mountain goat; however, as *Tosafos* implies, this does not match the behavioral descriptions given of the *tzvi*). Also, the *Yerushalmi* in *Eiruvin* 10a states that the horn of the *tzvi* is hollow. Both of these characteristics are possessed by the gazelle, which also matches the desciption of the alert and swift animal in Shir HaShirim.

28. See *Chiddushei Aggados*, vol. 2, p. 113.

29. Ibid.

30. Yehuda Feliks, *Nature and Man in the Bible* (Soncino Press, 1981), p. 153.

31. *Ta'anis* 3a.

32. *Bnei Yissachar*, Tishrei 13:4.

33. Cf. *Pri Tzaddik*, Shemini Atzeres 34.

34. See *Malbim* on Yirmeyahu 8:7.

35. It is almost universally accepted that the *chasidah* is the stork. In Iyov we find the verse "The wing of the ostrich waves joyously, but are they the feathers and plumage of the stork?" (Iyov 39:13). This description perfectly matches the stork, whose wings are black and white, like those of the ostrich, but far more spectacular (and actually functional). However, the *Torah Sheleimah* (on Vayikra 11:19) brings works such as *She'eilos U'Teshuvos HaRash* (20:20) and *Toldos Adam V'Chavah* (*Nesiv* 15), which cite a custom among certain Jews to eat storks, not considering it to be the non-kosher *chasidah* of the Torah. The *Beis Yosef* (on *Yoreh De'ah* 82:3), in a discussion on the topic of identifying birds, also cites Rabbeinu Yerucham, who had a tradition that the stork is a kosher bird. The justification is that the stork possesses all the signs of being kosher and is essentially similar to a duck; but, as the *Midrash Lekach Tov* points out, it is precisely because the *chasidah* appears to be kosher that the Torah had to mention it explicitly as being non-kosher.

36. *Chullin* 63a.

37. The other birds mentioned would also seem to relate to the themes of this month. The *tur*, "turtledove," is mentioned in the paragraph of Shir HaShirim we examined previously. The *sus*, "swift," and *agur*, "crane," are highlighted in Yeshayahu 38:14 as being especially vocal birds and would therefore relate to the themes of speech and song which are central to Nissan.

IYAR

1. Melachim I 6:1.

2. *Rosh HaShanah* 11a.

3. *Bnei Yissachar*, Iyar.

4. Ibid.

5. *Pri Tzaddik, sefer Vayikra*, p. 108.

6. *Midrash Tanchuma, Tazria* 5.

7. *Shir HaShirim Rabbah* 7:3.

8. See Shemos 34:29.

9. *Shem MiShmuel*, Pesach Sheini 5672.

10. *Yevamos* 61b.

11. *Kli Yakar*, Shemos 30:32.

12. *Nesivos Olam, Nesiv HaTorah* 1; see also the section "Form and Substance" in "Cheshvan."

13. *Yevamos* 62b.

14. *Nesivos Olam, Nesiv HaTorah* 12.

15. *Ta'anis* 6a; see *Rashi*.

16. *Bnei Yissachar.*

SIVAN

1. *Rashi*, Bereishis 8:22; see also *Ran* on *Nedarim* 61b.

2. For example, the forty-eight methods of acquiring Torah that are listed in *Avos* 6:6–7.

3. *Tiferes Yisrael* 3.

4. Maharal, *Tiferes Yisrael* 25.

5. *Shem MiShmuel, Ki Savo* 5676; see also the section "Toward Fruit" in "Shevat."

6. *Sifsei Chaim*, vol. 3, p. 149.

7. *"Vayigamel shekeidim"* (Bemidbar 17:24).

8. Rambam, *Hilchos Matnas Aniyim* 10:7.

9. *Shabbos* 31a.

10. *Rashi* loc. cit.

11. *Sifsei Chaim*, vol. 2, *"Middas HaChessed: Maftei'ach el HaTorah"*; see also the Introduction of this book; contrast the problems of *churban*, discussed in "Tamuz."

12. Melachim I 2:19, according to *Rashi*.

13. End of Rus.

14. *Rus Rabbah* 3:2.

15. *Sha'arei Teshuvah* on *Shulchan Aruch, Orach Chaim* 494:2, quoting *Rosh HaShanah* 11a.

16. *Or Gedalyahu, Mo'adim*, Chanukah 13; *Sifsei Chaim*, vol. 2, *"Megillas Rus: Chesed, Shoresh L'Malchus Beis David."*

17. The other insect to function as part of a *malchus* is the ant, called *nemalah*, which may be linked to the word *milah*, "word" (see *Rashi* on Bereishis 17:11 and Rabbi Shamshon Raphael Hirsch on Bereishis 25:29). Ants also have a system of communication: "Ants communicate by means of odors. They possess some half a dozen scent glands, each of which produces a 'fundamental concept' such as 'Alarm! Enemies entering nest!' or 'This track leads to the source of food.' Professor Edward O. Wilson, the American entomologist, has found indications that ants can combine several odors to make mixtures. In this way they possess more 'words' in their vocabulary than the mere number of scent glands in their bodies. Apparently these insects can also emit their signal odors at different rates of speed and modulate each emission so that odors of varying strengths result. Thus they create a kind of Morse code. Under these circumstances the existence of a form of sentence structure, though one very alien to our notions, is at least conceivable" (Vitus B. Droscher, *The Friendly Beast* [London: W. H. Allen & Company, 1970], p. 42).

TAMUZ

1. *Shem MiShmuel*, Tamuz 5672, citing Daniel 3:19; see also Yechezkel 8:14 and *Rashi* there.

2. See the section "Four Quarters" in the chapter "Dividing the Calendar."

3. *Bnei Yissachar.*

4. *Netzach Yisrael* 8.

5. *Ta'anis* 26a.

6. *Bereishis Rabbah* 34:11; *Seforno* on Bereishis 8:22; see also *Malbim,* Bereishis 8:22.

7. This explanation, by Rabbi Simchah Wasserman, is cited in *Reb Simcha Speaks* (Artscroll), p.103.

8. *Or Gedalyahu, Mo'adim*, Purim 2.

9. *Ka'as* is often identified as a waterside bird, such as a pelican (*Shabbos* 21a). However, based on this *pasuk*'s description of it living in a desert habitat, Ibn Janach points out that this does not seem likely. It may refer to the desert subspecies of the little owl, *Athene noctua saharae*. More recent discoveries, however, have shown that there are indeed seabirds living in deserts. The garuma gull, *larus modestus*, nests in the oppressively hot Atacama desert of Chile, twenty miles from the sea. No one knows why it does this.

10. *Targum Yonasan* on Vayikra 11:17; *Rashi; R' Saadiah Gaon; Ibn Janach*; however, see *Beis Yosef* to *Yoreh De'ah* 82:3.

11. *Rashi* on Tehillim 102:6–7.

12. *Targum Yonasan* on Tehillim 102:6–7.

13. *Niddah* 23a.

14. See *Zohar, parashas Shelach.*

15. *Shem MiShmuel,* Tamuz 5672.

16. Yechezkel 8:14.

17. *Shem MiShmuel, Tazria* 5675; Sukkos 5679.

18. *Maharsha* on *Ta'anis* 4a.

19. Reb Tzadok, *Takanas HaShavin, Likutei inyanei teshuvah l'shavei pesha b'Yaakov,* s.v. *"u'birur zeh."*

20. *Shem MiShmuel,* Tamuz 5672.

AV

1. *Netzach Yisrael* 55.

2. *Eichah Rabbah; Yerushalmi, Berachos.*

3. Daniel 4:34.

4. *Ri Migash* on *Bava Basra* 93a.

5. Rabbi Chaim Kanievsky, commentary on *Perek Shirah.*

6. See *Ta'anis* 29a.

7. Cf. *Pri Tzaddik,* Tamuz 4.

8. *Abarbanel,* Yeshayahu 5:1–7.

9. Ibid.

10. Ibid.

11. *Vayikra Rabbah* 36:2; *Midrash Shmuel* 16:1.

12. Ibid.

13. See commentaries on Yeshayahu 5:1–7; see also *Kenaf Renanim,* "Gefen."

14. *Kenaf Renanim,* "Gefen."

15. *Vayikra Rabbah* 13:5.

16. Rabbi Yaakov Emden, commentary on *Perek Shirah.*

17. *Ta'anis* 30b.

18. See Shoftim, ch. 19–21.

19. Rambam, *Hilchos Talmud Torah* 3:13.

20. The Gemara explains "being gathered in before one's time" as meaning "being buried by one's mother." This seemingly bizarre statement can perhaps be understood by looking at the broader pattern in the year that we have been describing. Spring is the time of the nation's birth, when we only receive from Hashem and share a child-parent relationship with Him. As we enter the winter section of the year, and the festival of Sukkos in particular, we relate to Hashem as our "husband" instead. Being His partner in this type of relationship, we have obligations we are expected to fulfill, the prime example of which is studying Torah. On Tu B'Av, which heralds the winter section of the year, one must increase one's study of Torah and thereby begin to enter into the new type of relationship, with all its demands. Someone who fails to do this has demonstrated an inability to grow out of the old, dependent relationship; thus "his mother buries him." Perhaps this also gives us an insight into why the Mishnah states that a child is obligated in the mitzvah of sukkah (which, as we shall see, represents a huband-wife relationship with Hashem) from the time he is independant of his mother (*Sukkah* 2:8).

21. *Bnei Yissachar.*

ELUL

1. Cf. *Shem MiShmuel*, Sukkos 5672.

2. *Pri Tzaddik*, Elul 4.

3. See *Rashi, Bava Metzia* 38a, s.v. *"hidvish."*

4. *Gevuros Hashem* 43.

5. *Or Gedalyahu, Mo'adim*, Elul 2.

6. *Beis Elokim.*

TISHREI

1. *Yalkut Shimoni* 5:42.

2. *Sifsei Chaim*, vol. 1, p. 93.

3. *Shem MiShmuel*, Sukkos 5672.

4. *Vayikra Rabbah* 30:12.

5. Maharal, *Gevuros Hashem* 46.

6. Vayikra 23:39.

7. See *Rashi* on Shemos 34:22.

8. *Seder Olam*.

9. See *Sefas Emes*, Sukkos 5648.

10. *Sefas Emes*.

11. Vayikra 23:40, Devarim 16:14, and Devarim 16:15.

12. *Shem MiShmuel*, Sukkos 5678; see *Bnei Yissachar, Ma'amarei Tishrei* 10:22, for a contrast of *simchah* with *sasson*.

13. Bereishis 4:1.

14. Cf. *Shem MiShmuel*, Simchas Torah 5681.

15. *Ben Yehoyada* on *Ta'anis* 6b.

CHESHVAN

1. *Tosafos, Shabbos* 31a, quoting *Yerushalmi*.

2. *Or Gedalyahu, Shemos* 2.

3. *Rashi* on Tehillim 92:3.

4. *Berachos* 33b.

5. *Aderes Eliyahu, V'Zos HaBerachah*.

6. *Ta'anis* 6a.

7. *Rashi* on Bereishis 6:17.

8. *Midrash Tehillim* 1:18.

9. Ibid.

10. Ibid.

11. *Ta'anis* 7a.

12. *Midrash Tehillim* 1:18.

13. Ibid.

14. Ibid.

15. *Or Gedalyahu, parashas Noach*.

16. *Bava Basra* 74a; see *Anaf Yosef* (in *Ein Yaakov*) to *Yoma* 54b.

17. *Yalkut Shimoni* on Melachim 1:6.

18. *Bnei Yissachar*, Cheshvan 1.

KISLEV

1. One might ask why the Biblically prescribed *Yamim Nora'im* and Sukkos are in Tishrei, which is in the winter section of the year. The answer is that the split is indeed uneven. One of Hashem's thirteen attributes of mercy is "great in kindness," which means that He tilts the scales in favor of kindness (*Rosh HaShanah* 17a). Thus, the summer order of *chesed* extends into the winter order of *din*, mitigating it to produce *rachamim*. Cf. *Rashi* on *Ta'anis* 3b, s.v. "*bimos hachamah.*"

2. *Pri Tzaddik*, Chanukah 4.

3. Rabbi Yonasan Eibeshitz, in *Ye'aros Devash* (*derush* 15), explains that Adam HaRishon was not ignorant of the solar system's workings. Rather, he had originally been in Gan Eden, which is on the equator and has days and nights of equal length. When he sinned, Hashem drove him north, and he thought he would be driven to the North Pole, where there is no daylight during the winter.

4. Maharal, *Ner Mitzvah*.

5. Cf. *Sifsei Chaim*, vol. 2, p. 61.

6. *Pachad Yitzchak*, Chanukah 7.

7. Malbim on Hoshea 14:7. *Hod* is translated by the *Targum* as *ziv* (see "Iyar"). The full translation of this phrase in the *Targum* is ויהי כזיו מנחת קודשא זיוהון.

8. *Rokeach*, *Hilchos Chanukah* 225.

9. *Bnei Yissachar*, Kislev 4:86.

10. See *Ner Mitzvah* and its explanation in *Bnei Yissachar*, Kislev 4:86–113, which states that a different calendar system is the basis for this.

11. *Bnei Yissachar*, Kislev 3:1.

12. The word *brazen* also refers to something made out of brass, a strong alloy of copper. In another prophetic vision, Yavan was represented by copper. (See *Ner Mitzvah*, p. 16.)

13. *Ner Mitzvah*.

14. *Or Gedalyahu*, Chanukah 5.

15. *Shem MiShmuel*, Chanukah 5673, sixth night; *Or Gedalyahu*, Chanukah 5, 6.

16. *Rabbeinu Yonah* on *Avos* 2:5.

17. *Orach Chaim* 1.

18. *Beis Yosef.*

19. *Tzidkas HaTzaddik* 167; *Dover Tzedek, mitzvos asei* 1; *Kometz HaMinchah* 2:6.

20. *Yerushalmi, Yevamos* 48b.

21. Rabbi Shamshon Raphael Hirsch, commentary to *parashas Terumah* on the Menorah.

22. Cf. *Shem MiShmuel*, Mikeitz 5680.

23. *Vayikra Rabbah* 13:5.

24. *Pri Tzaddik*, Kislev 4; *Or Gedalyahu, Mo'adim*, Purim 7

25. *Ramban*, Shemos 13:16; Rabbi Yaakov Emden, Introduction to *Sulam*.

TEVES

1. See *Or Gedalyahu, Mo'adim*, Chanukah 16.

2. *Megillas Ta'anis, Tosafos Chadashim*, citing *Kol Bo*.

3. *Ta'anis* 29a.

4. See the section "Four Quarters" in the chapter "Dividing the Calendar."

5. *Shem MiShmuel*, Sukkos 5679, *Tazria* 5675.

6. *Zohar* 1:238b.

7. See also *Shem MiShmuel*, Rosh Chodesh Teves 5623, which states that each kingdom acquired the power of those preceding it.

8. *Shem MiShmuel*, Rosh Chodesh Teves 5673.

9. The Midrash on this verse (*Bereishis Rabbah* 65:15) sees it as an allusion to Yeshayahu's prophecies concerning the destruction of Bavel: "Therefore, I will make the heavens tremble... Bavel...shall never be inhabited... The goats shall leap around there..." (Yeshayahu 13:13–21).

10. *Pri Tzaddik*, Rosh Chodesh Teves 18.

11. Interestingly, the brazen leopard and the brazen goat are always presented as a predator-prey pair. For example: "The wolf shall dwell with the lamb, and the leopard with the goat..." (Yeshayahu 11:6); "The goat is the prey of the leopard" (*Vayikra Rabbah* 27:5). We also find that the leopard statue was placed opposite the goat on the steps of Shlomo HaMelech's throne, being its *tamei* counterpart (*Midrash Abba Gurion* 1).

12. *Pri Tzaddik*, Rosh Chodesh Teves 18.

13. The simple understanding of the Gemara is that it refers to one's good inclination trembling with *rage* over the evil inclination; however, *Pri Tzaddik*
(Rosh Chodesh Teves 18) explains it to mean trembling in fear, as is the understanding of *Rashi* and several other commentaries on the cited verse.

14. *Pri Tzaddik*, Rosh Chodesh Teves 18.

15. Maharal, *Or Chadash*, Esther 2:16.

SHEVAT

1. *Rosh HaShanah* 14a.

2. *Rashi* on *Rosh HaShanah* 14a.

3. *Yerushalmi, Rosh HaShanah* 1:2.

4. *Or Gedalyahu, sefer Shemos*, Shevat.

5. *Midrash Tehillim* 1:18.

6. *Bnei Yissachar.*

7. Shemos 2:19.

8. *Tiferes Yisrael* 43; cf. *Or HaChaim* and *Kli Chemdah* on the beginning of *sefer Devarim.*

9. *Or Gedalyahu, sefer Shemos*, Shevat.

10. *Pri Tzaddik*, Shevat 3.

11. Cf. Maharal, *Chiddushei Aggados*, vol. 1, p. 105.

12. Ibid.

13. Rabbi Chaim Shmuelevitz, *Sichos Mussar* 5731:5.

14. *Rashi, Metzudas David*, and *Malbim* on Tehillim 92:8.

15. *Metzudas David* and *Seforno* on Tehillim 92:13–15.

16. Maharal, *Gevuros Hashem*, ch. 29.

17. Maharal, *Gevuros Hashem*, ch. 11, 37.

18. See Bereishis 13:10 and *Rashi* there.

19. The inclusion of wheat is not at odds with our description of Eretz Yisrael as a
land of fruit, for, as we already noted, wheat originally grew in the form of a
fruit-bearing tree. The inclusion of barley, however, does require further study.

20. Maharal, *Chiddushei Aggados*, vol. 1, p. 105.

21. Rabbi Shamshon Raphael Hirsch, *The Jewish Year*, "Shevat II."

22. *Ramban*, Introduction to *sefer Shemos*. I have heard it suggested that it was for this reason that the Sadducees wanted to count the *omer* from the Sunday after Pesach rather than from Pesach itself. Counting the *omer* from Pesach links Pesach to Shavuos, indicating that the independence from Egypt is only of value insofar as it was a means for our accepting the Torah. There is no value to rejuvenation and freedom unless there is a purpose to them — the ability to better serve Hashem.

ADAR

1. The events of megillas Esther are recorded as occurring in the twelfth month, though it was actually in the second Adar (*Birkas Chaim*).

2. Bereishis 48:5.

3. *Or Gedalyahu, sefer Shemos, parashas Vayakhel-Pekudei.*

4. *Ner Mitzvah*, p. 11.

5. Mishlei 17:12.

6. See *Radak* on Hoshea 13:8.

7. *Yisrael Kedoshim* 9.

8. The word *dov* actually means "movement"; consider the phrase *sefasayim dovevos*, "murmuring lips."

9. *Vayikra Rabbah* 13:5.

10. Ezra 1:2.

11. *Bereishis Rabbah* 63:10.

12. *Orach Chaim* 694:3.

13. *Pachad Yitzchak*, Purim 16.

14. *Rashi* on Devarim 25:18.

15. *Or Gedalyahu, Mo'adim*, Purim 7.

16. The letter *tzaddi* is a stronger-sounding version of the letter *sin* and is therefore a different version of the same basic concept.

17. Rabbi Shamshon Raphael Hirsch, *Jewish Symbolism*, p. 213.

18. *Sar Shalom*, brought in *Me'am Loez* on Shir HaShirim 2:11.

APPENDIX A
FRACTAL MATHEMATICS

The emerging science of fractal mathematics is of enormous significance. In these pages, we shall explore it in greater depth.

Science

For several hundred years preceding this century, science had been diverging from Torah, with theories such as the static universe model and the general idea of absolute determinism in nature. But with the vast increase in scientific knowledge of this century, the trend has changed. Since Torah is the blueprint of creation, as scientific knowledge becomes a more perfect description of creation it becomes more similar to Torah. With ever-increasing rapidity, science is converging with Torah.

There are many specific examples of this phenomenon, some of which are discussed later. But let us take a step back to look at the big picture and survey the essence of what is taking place.

Mathematics

Science tries to explain various aspects of the universe in formulae we can understand and work with. The result is a set of mathematical equations which describe the universe. This may not strike us as being particularly significant. But consider the following statement by Morris Kline in *Mathematics and the Physical World* (New York: Dover, 1980, ix):

> A study of mathematics and its contributions to the sciences exposes a deep

question. Mathematics is man-made. The concepts, the broad ideas, the logical standards and methods of reasoning...were fashioned by human beings. Yet with the product of his fallible mind, man has surveyed spaces too vast for his imagination to encompass; he has predicted and shown how to control radio waves which none of our senses can perceive; and he has discovered particles too small to be seen with the most powerful microscope... Some explanation of this marvelous power is called for.

Many people are beginning to express astonishment at the fact that there is order to the universe, order that our minds can grasp. To the Torah Jew, it is a source of wonder but not of surprise. Since the universe was created with direction, following a plan, it is only "natural" that there should be *seder*, "order," to the universe.

The recent advances in science are steps toward recognizing the unity of the universe. Very little scientific progress has ever been made by polytheistic cultures. Seeing the universe as being controlled by a variety of disparate powers, there is no reason to search for global scientific laws. Today's scientific theories describing the universe, which will hopefully soon be united in a grand unified theory, is leading up to an acknowledgment of a Creator. For why should the universe make so much sense if there is no designer? This point was expressed by Albert Einstein in *Lettres a Maurice Solovine* (Paris: Gauthier Villars, 1956, p. 102):

> You find it surprising that I think of the comprehensibility of the world...as a miracle or eternal mystery. But surely, *a priori*, one should expect the world to be chaotic, not to be grasped by thought in any way.

Fractals

Until recently, there was considerable doubt about the effectiveness of mathematics in describing real-life phenomena. Mathematics was thought to be limited to mathematical models, which are only approximations of real life. Mathematics was entirely linear in nature, while real-life phenomena such as plants and fluid flow were non-linear. The objects of geometry were regular squares and perfect circles; they could never be jagged-edged leaves and flowing streams.

With the advent of fractal mathematics, all this changed. Fractals presented a new way of looking at nature — not in terms of absolute dimensions, but in terms of patterns. This is one of the ways the Torah uses to describe the universe. In many areas of the Torah, we find no mention of absolute measurements, only of patterns and rules. (Incidentally, this is an enormously space-saving procedure. Instead of describing an entire structure or series of structures, one need only know the rules that are used in creating it.)

Thus, instead of trying to describe the height and shape of a whole plant, we now look at a certain pattern which is expressed in each leaf and which continually unfolds as the plant grows. For that *is* the mechanism of growth — taking the pattern, taking the formula, and further applying it. It is the same system Hashem used when He created the worlds. He took the pattern — the Torah — and continually implemented it further until our world was produced (see Introduction).

The Mandelbrot Set

This brings us to the most intriguing aspect of fractals, the Mandelbrot set, named after its discoverer, Benoit Mandelbrot.

The Mandelbrot set is a very small code: $z \rightarrow z^2 + c$, where z is a complex number. When the numbers are inserted into this equation, and the results are plotted as graphics, the outcome is extraordinary. A strange picture emerges of bizarre shapes with spirals and spikes. When this picture is magnified, none of the detail is lost. More spirals and spikes are observed. As one continues to magnify the picture, similar patterns will be noticed, but *never actually the same*. This small code produces a world of infinite detail.

This is a perfect analogy to the Torah itself, which is a relatively tiny code, yet produces the infinitely detailed universe in which we live.

APPENDIX B

TORAH AND DNA

The parallels between Torah and DNA are intriguing. In this section, we shall explore them in a little more depth.

The Source of Life

Both Torah and DNA are the source of life. The Torah is seen as the root of all existence. At a physical level, DNA is considered the most basic requirement for the formation of life.

Instructions for Life

The word *torah* means "teaching," for the Torah is the instruction book not only for ourselves but for the entire universe. DNA is the instruction code for organizing amino acids into living organisms. The first part of the DNA sequence contains instructions for reading the rest of the instructions! Looking back, it might be obvious that a genetic instruction code is needed, but *a priori* it was not expected at all. Life was expected to simply *be*, without the need for actual physical instructions.

Form of Code

The Torah is a linear sequence of letters. DNA, too, is a linear sequence of molecules and not the complex map or architect's blueprint of a body one might expect.

Components of Code

The Torah is composed of the letters of *Lashon HaKodesh*, the Hebrew alphabet. These are the raw material of Creation, the building blocks of the spiritual and physical worlds. There are twenty-two letters in the Hebrew alphabet.

DNA works in the same way. In the words of microbiologist Dr. Michael Denton: "The linear sequence of amino acids in a protein can be thought of as a sentence made up of a long combination of the amino acid letters. Just as different sentences are made up of different sequences of letters, so different proteins are made up of different sequences of amino acids." There are twenty-two amino acids used by DNA in the construction of physical life. (Most textbooks say twenty, but there are in fact two additional amino acids which are rarely found.)

Compression of Data

Seeing as the Torah is the code for the entire universe, it is amazingly short. Every particle, every thought, every action of all space and time is in the Torah — if you know where to look. This density of information is achieved through many different techniques, one of which we shall soon explore.

DNA, too, is a remarkably compact code. Each strand of DNA contains every aspect of the person, including the hundreds of millions of sensors in our eyes, the innumerable neural connections in our brains, and our fingerprint patterns. With ordinary data-storage procedures, such a vast code would have to contain *trillions* of words. Yet DNA accomplishes all this with only a few hundred million words.

Systems of Compression

Both Torah and DNA use similar systems of compression. In the Torah, there are certain principles of how to extract further information from other sections of data. For example, a *gezeirah shaveh* transfers laws from one concept to another. The information itself is translated into new forms of information. Other principles, too, may be applied. The end result is that we see the Torah contains a far greater amount of information than we thought at first glance.

The same is true for DNA. The original proteins have a specific set of functions. After performing these functions, the proteins are broken down into smaller proteins, which perform entirely different functions. Afterward, these too break down. Again, the end result is that there was much more genetic information present than a first look at the molecules indicated.

Another way in which the Torah compresses information is through the superimposition of different sets of data. This means that by splitting up the sequence of letters in the Torah differently, different words emerge. Take the very first verse of the Torah:

...בראשית ברא

In the beginning, He created...

...ברא שית ברא

He created six [worlds]...

...בראש יתברא

At first, He will create...

Splitting up these letters can be done in a multitude of different ways, to reveal different messages; our version of the Torah is the one suited for us.

The identical method of compressing data is used by DNA. Different messages are overlapped or superimposed, such that by splitting up the sequence in different ways, the different messages are revealed.

Books on this subject give parables to explain this concept. One example uses Morse code to demonstrate the point:

Letter	Morse Code
A	•—
I	• •
M	— —
N	— •

Overlapping Messages:

M A N A

__ __ •__ __• •__ • • •

M   I N I

This is a simple example, given to show how enough code for five letters when written normally can contain many more letters when the words overlap. The books find it difficult to find more accurate examples of greater compression. However, the sample we have shown from the Torah does exactly that, achieving a 100-percent overlap.

For the secular scientific world, this extraordinary system of data storage came as a great shock. *Omni* magazine asked the prestigious Royal Society of Great Britain to list the most sensational scientific advances of the 1970s. One of the prime candidates was the first decoding of a DNA sequence, that of a simple virus codenamed PhiX-174. The magazine reported as follows:

> Quite a perplexing revelation from this work was that the genes actually overlap. Like a telegram with no spacing, the coded message read entirely differently, depending upon whether one began with the first, second, or third letter. The fact that three messages were contained within one seemed to some researchers artificial or contrived, prompting Drs. Hiromitsu Yokoo and Iairo Oshima to revise the theory, first suggested by Dr. Francis Crick and Leslie Orgel (*Icarus*, Vol. 19, 1973, p. 341) that life on Earth began from organisms that were sent here billions of years ago by extraterrestrial civilizations that decided to "seed" other planets.

Faced with the unbelievable level of design in DNA, yet too afraid to confront the obvious conclusion, the scientists were forced to conclude that DNA was produced by extraterrestrial intelligence.

APPENDIX C
THE FLOW OF TIME

In Search of the Perfect Line

We learned that the orbital path of the Earth, by which we measure time, is a physical manifestation of the flow of spiritual time. We referred to this flow as "cyclical," meaning that it repeats itself in a continual cycle. This is not true to an absolute degree. If time flowed along a perfectly circular or elliptical path, history would continually repeat itself exactly (which is in fact how the ancient Greeks viewed time). In truth, the cycle repeats itself in terms of a general pattern, never exactly the same, yet following the same guidelines.

Many people try to find the perfect geometrical description of the flow of time. A spiral is a better description than a circle, and a helix better still. But for the most accurate description of the spiritual flow of time, we need only utilize the principle that everything spiritual has a physical reflection and analyze the Earth's orbit more closely.

Recent studies in astronomy and chaos mathematics indicate that the same pattern we have described for the flow of spiritual time is true of the Earth's orbit. In this section, we shall explore this pattern. If this information is true, it demonstrates a perfect parallel between physical time and spiritual time; if not, it will serve as an excellent model for understanding the flow of spiritual time.

In a highly simplified model of the universe, containing only the Earth and the sun, represented by point masses, the Earth's orbit would repeat itself exactly. The only force of gravity it would be subject to would be that of the sun. The real universe, however, is vastly different. The Earth is not a point mass. There are gravitational pulls on the Earth from the moon and the other planets in the solar system. These effects are dwarfed by the force exerted by the vast bulk of the sun, but they still exist.

The apparent effect of these other bodies is remarkable. The path of the Earth's orbit, continually subject to minute tugging, follows a slightly chaotic path. The result is a line that stays in an approximately elliptical shape, but *never actually crosses itself.* It was discovered that an infinitely long line can be enclosed within a finite volume. So an infinitely long orbital path can be enclosed within a torus (bagel shape). The practical upshot of all this is that the Earth is never in exactly the same place twice. The implications of this model for spiritual time are clear: it means that while each year is not an exact rerun of the previous year, it will nevertheless follow the same general pattern.

The Accumulation of Orbits

There is another relevant aspect of this line. As the number of orbits increase, they collectively form a torus. The surface of this shape is continually refined with each orbit. What is originally a rather messy shape will, after many revolutions, become an ever more perfect geometrical shape.

History progresses the same way. At each point in time there is a unique *tikkun* (spiritual rectification) to be made. Each year adds to Hashem's grand cosmic plan for bringing the world to perfection. In some years, this will be easy to perceive. In years of suffering, it will be more difficult to perceive. But when history reaches its climax with the coming of Mashiach, we will be able to look back at the history of the world and see how every stage was a vital step toward reaching the final stage of perfection.

Slices of Time

There is one more remarkable feature of this line. Imagine a slice taken of this orbit. In other words, imagine a giant piece of paper held at one point in the orbit, such that at a particular date each year, the Earth passes through it, making a tiny hole. Now, one would expect the result to be a random mess of holes. After all, the points on this cross section fall in a random manner, impossible to predict. In fact, the points progressively reveal a pattern. A coherent shape will be revealed with ever-increasing detail with every passage of an orbit.

This parallels the concept of the calendar precisely. Each point in the year has to be seen in terms of that point in every year during history. Pesach can be understood in its full depth only with the consideration of every Pesach that has transpired and will transpire during history. Together, they form a pattern in time, a coherent picture of a *mo'ed*, a rendezvous with Hashem of a particular type.

TIME CYCLES
AND CHARTS

Time Cycle I: The Division of the Year

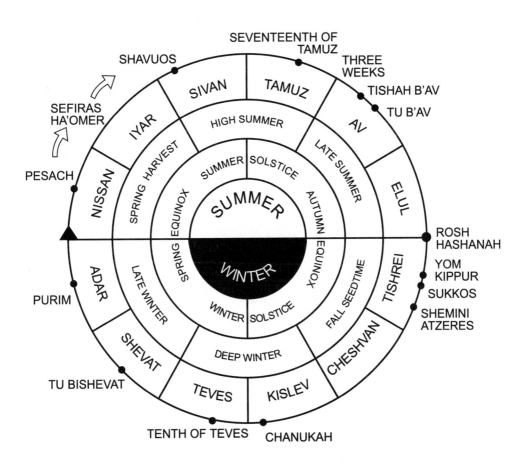

Time Cycle II: The Symmetry of the Year

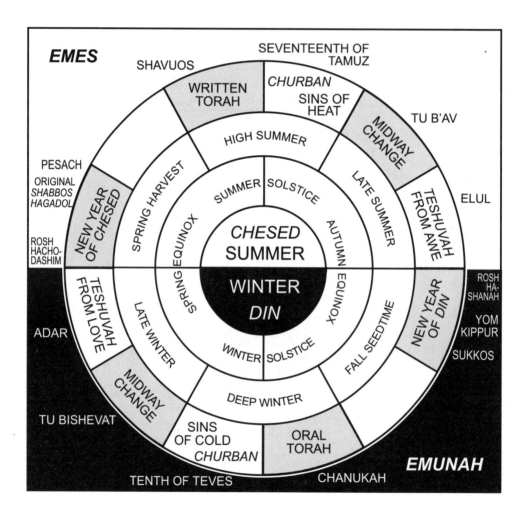

The year possesses mirror symmetry. Each element in the year has its counterpart in the opposite part of the year. See, for example, "Advance and Withdrawal" in "Elul" and "Fire and Ice" in "Teves."

Chart I: The Purpose and Pattern of Torah

Manifestation between Man and Man   *Manifestation between Man and Hashem*

CHUMASH	COMMANDMENTS	DEVELOPMENT	COMMANDMENTS	CHUMASH
Bereishis Value of the individual	**"Do Not Murder"** Other people's right to exist; value of life	**Stage One** Acceptance of others' existence	**Accepting Hashem** Acceptance of Hashem's existence	**Bereishis** Existence of Hashem
Shemos Property laws (*Mishpatim*)	**"Do Not Commit Adultery"** Accepting other's ownership of wife	**Stage Two** Acceptance of their rights of ownership	**"Do Not Worship Idols"** Hashem's ownership of all universe	**Shemos** Acceptance of Hashem as God by the Jewish people
Vayikra Acceptance of the laws	**"Do Not Steal [Kidnap]"** No unlawful use of another's being, person, or property	**Stage Three** No unlawful use of property (lawful coexistence)	**"Do Not Take Hashem's Name in Vain"** No unlawful use of Hashem's Name	**Vayikra** Acceptance of the laws
Bemidbar Organization of the nation; cooperation in war	**"Do Not Testify Falsely"** No destructive talk; hence, cooperate	**Stage Four** Readiness to cooperate	**Observing Shabbos** Testifying to Hashem's authority	**Bemidbar** Sanctification of the people
Devarim Projected unity with the nation	**"Do Not Covet"** No resentment of others	**Stage Five** Total unity	**Honoring Parents** Unity with one's source	**Devarim** Projected unity with Hashem

Chart II: The Zodiac

MONTH	ZODIAC	*MAZAL*	DEFINITION
Nissan	Aries	*Taleh*	The lamb
Iyar	Taurus	*Shor*	The ox
Sivan	Gemini	*Te'umim*	Twins
Tamuz	Cancer	*Sartan*	The crab
Av	Leo	*Aryeh*	The lion
Elul	Virgo	*Besulah*	The virgin
Tishrei	Libra	*Moznayim*	Scales
Cheshvan	Scorpio	*Akrav*	The scorpion
Kislev	Sagittarius	*Keshes*	The bow
Teves	Capricorn	*Gedi*	The goat
Shevat	Aquarius	*D'li*	The bucket
Adar	Pisces	*Dagim*	Fish

GLOSSARY

Adam HaRishon:	Adam; the first man.
Amidah:	Prayer recited three times daily.
Aryeh:	Lion.
Azus:	Brazenness.
Bavel:	Babylon.
Beis HaMikdash:	The Holy Temple.
Bemidbar:	The book of Numbers.
Berachah:	Blessing.
Bereishis:	The book of Genesis.
Bnei Yisrael:	The children of Israel.
Bnei Yissachar:	Mystical work on the Jewish year.
Chag:	Festival.
Chesed:	Kindness.
Chol HaMo'ed:	The intermediate days of Pesach and Sukkos.
Chomer:	Substance; opposite of *tzurah*.
Chovos HaLevavos:	Eleventh-century philosophical work by Rabbeinu Bachya ibn Pekuda.
Chumash:	The five books of the Torah.
Churban:	Destruction; specifically the destruction of the Temples.
Devarim:	The book of Deuteronomy.
Din:	Judgment.
Edom:	Empire descended from Eisav.

Eisav:	Esau.
Emunah:	Faith; faithfulness.
Eretz Yisrael:	The Land of Israel.
Gevuros Hashem:	Work on the Exodus by Maharal.
Kiddush Levanah:	Prayer recited to sanctify the new moon.
Korban:	Offering.
Gan Eden:	The Garden of Eden.
Galus:	Exile.
Gemara:	The Talmud.
Geulah:	Redemption.
Har Sinai:	Mount Sinai.
Hashem:	Literally, "the name"; God.
Hoshana Rabbah:	Seventh day of the Sukkos festival.
Kenaf Renanim:	Commentary on *Perek Shirah* by Rabbi Chanoch Zundel Luria, published in Krotoschin in 1842.
Koheles:	The book of Ecclesiastes; alternative name for its author, King Solomon.
Madai:	The ancient kingdom of Media.
Maharal:	Rabbi Yehudah Loewe ben Betzalel of Prague (c.1512–1609), author of numerous philosophical/mystical works.
Mashiach:	Messiah.
Matzah:	Unleavened bread.
Michtav MeEliyahu:	Collected philosophical discourses and writings of Rabbi Eliyahu Dessler (1891–1954) of Russia, London, and Bnei Brak.
Mitzrayim:	Egypt.
Mizbei'ach:	The Altar.
Mo'ed (mo'adim):	Literally, "rendezvous"; festival(s).

Ner Mitzvah:	Work on Chanukah by Maharal.
Or Gedalyahu:	Collected discourses of Rabbi Gedalyah Schorr, late dean of Yeshivas Torah VaDa'as in Brooklyn, on the *Chumash* and the festivals.
Omer:	See SEFIRAS HA'OMER.
Paras:	The ancient kingdom of Persia.
Perek Shirah:	Ancient text that lists animals, plants, and other features of the natural world, assigning a verse to each of them. The verse alludes to the philosophical or ethical lesson that is manifest by the creature.
Pesach:	Passover.
Pri Tzaddik:	Mystical work by Rabbi Tzadok HaKohen Rabinowitz of Lublin (1823–1900) on the *Chumash* and the festivals.
Rachamim:	Mercy.
Rambam:	Rabbi Moshe ben Maimon (1135–1204); Maimonides.
Rosh Chodesh:	The first day of the new lunar month.
Sefer Yetzirah:	The Book of Creation, an ancient Kabbalistic work.
Sefiras ha'omer:	The counting of days from the second day of Pesach, when the *omer* offering is brought, until Shavuos.
Shabbos:	Sabbath.
Shavuos:	The Festival of Pentecost.
Shem MiShmuel:	Mystical work on the *Chumash* and the Jewish year by Rabbi Shmuel Bornstein of Sochatchov (1856–1926).
Shemini Atzeres:	Festival celebrated eight days from the beginning of Sukkos.
Shemos:	The book of Exodus.
Shir HaShirim:	The book of Song of Songs.
Shirah:	Song.
Shlomo HaMelech:	King Solomon.
Shemittah:	The sabbatical year.
Sifsei Chaim:	Contemporary work on the Jewish year in three volumes authored by the late Rabbi Chaim Friedlander of Bnei Brak.

Simchah: Joy.

Simchas Torah: Festival celebrating the completion of the cycle of reading the Torah, held on Shemini Atzeres in Eretz Yisrael and on the following day in the Diaspora.

Techiyas hameisim: The resurrection of the dead.

Tiferes Yisrael: Work on Shavuos and the Torah by Maharal.

Tu BiShevat: The fifteenth of Shevat, the New Year for trees.

Tur: Fifteenth-century work on Jewish law.

Tzurah: Form; opposite of *chomer.*

Vayikra: The book of Leviticus.

Yaakov: Jacob.

Yavan: The ancient empire of Greece.

Zohar: Ancient Kabbalistic text.

Zeman: Time.